A TASTE
OF ENGLAND
THE WEST COUNTRY

Traditional Food

Theodora FitzGibbon

Period photographs compiled and
prepared by George Morrison

Pan Books London and Sydney

Also by Theodora FitzGibbon
in Pan Books

A Taste of Scotland
A Taste of Ireland
A Taste of Wales
A Taste of London
A Taste of Paris
A Taste of Yorkshire

Crockery Pot Cooking

For all my friends of the West Country,
particularly my friend of many years,
Yvonne Chudleigh, with love and thanks
for all their kindness,
encouragement and help

First published 1972 by J. M. Dent & Sons Ltd
This edition published 1975 by Pan Books Ltd,
Cavaye Place, London SW10 9PG
5th printing 1980
ISBN 0 330 24364 0
© Theodora FitzGibbon 1972
Permission to reproduce the specially prepared photographs
for any purpose must be obtained from the author
Printed in Great Britain by Fletcher & Son Ltd, Norwich

ACKNOWLEDGMENTS

Our thanks are due to all the friends who have helped us in the research for this book, particularly Lord Weymouth for talking to us about the West Country, of which both he and his family are so much a part: to his father, the Marquess of Bath, for the loan of family photographs. To Lord and Lady Digby, for their kindness, and the loan of family photographs. Miss Frances FitzGibbon for putting us in touch with a true Wiltshire countrywoman, Mrs Petherbridge, who kindly lent her old recipe book, some of which appears in the following pages. To Mr H. L. Douch B.A., Curator of the Royal Institution of Cornwall, Truro, for all his kindness, and the valuable information he gave us. The Misses Hamblin of the Natural History Museum, Torquay, for giving up part of their holiday to see us. Mr and Mrs Blackmore of Minehead who provided an invaluable photograph; Mr K. Lloyd Plumridge of the Wyndham Museum, Yeovil, who went to immense trouble to locate certain photographs. Mr and Mrs Maurice Moriarty, Miss Aileen Hamilton and Mr and Mrs Anthony Ward for their help in many ways. Also to Mr Richard Larn, the author, who allowed us to choose freely from his collection.

I wish to thank the following people for their kindness, patience and valuable assistance: Miss Harris of the Gloucester Central Public Library; Mr Brian S. Smith of the Gloucester Records Office; Mrs Pringle of Cheltenham Public Libraries; Mr Peter Pagan, Miss John and Mr Kite of the Bath Municipal Libraries; Mr G. Langley of the Bristol Central Public Libraries and Mr Paul Elkin of Bristol City Museum, both of whom went to great trouble; Mr G. Noakes and Mr P. R. Saunders of the Salisbury and South Wiltshire Museum; Mr K. Carter and Miss Simons of Dorset County Library; Miss C. Hawkridge and Mr Colin Edwards of the Truro Records Office; Miss Semmens of Penzance Public Library; and particularly, Mr Stone of Exeter Public Library, whose vast knowledge of his collection, and kindness, gave us some really superb results; Miss Goodson and Mr Hollier of Bridgwater County Library; Dr Wallis of Wells Museum; Mr D. B. Thomas, of the Science Museum, London, and Mr F. Gibson, Isles of Scilly, for permission to use some of his photographs. Photographs on pages viii, 13, 33, 57, 85 are reproduced by kind permission of the Gloucester Public Library; on pages 81, 117, by kind permission of the Gloucester Records Office, and Mrs Albino; on page 27 by courtesy of Cheltenham Public Library; on pages 19, 87, by kind permission of the Bath Municipal Library; on pages 31, 115, by kind permission of Bristol Central Public Libraries; on pages 23, 51, by kind permission of Bristol City Museum and Art Gallery; on pages 3, 9, 43, 71, 89, 103, by kind permission of the Salisbury and South Wiltshire Museum; on pages 39, 55, 61, 67, 73, 77, by courtesy of Dorset County Library, O. N. Martin, Esquire, and Mrs L. A. Keith Hall; on pages 75, 99, 101, by kind permission of Borough of Yeovil Wyndham Museum; on pages 21, 109, by kind permission of Truro Records Office; on page 59, by kind permission of the Royal Institution of Cornwall, Truro; on page 91, by kind permission of Helston Museum; on pages 45, 69, by kind permission of Penzance Public Library and Mr F. Gibson; on pages 11, 15, 25, 37, 41, 47, 53, 79, 107, 111, by kind permission of Exeter Public Libraries; on page 29, by courtesy of Torquay Natural History Museum; on pages 7, 49, 95, by kind permission of Bridgwater County Library; on pages 5, 63, 113, by kind permission of Wells Museum; on page 105, by courtesy of Mr D. B. Thomas, of the Science Museum, London; on page 83, by kind permission of Mr Blackmore; on page 97, by kind permission of Mr Richard Larn and Mr F. Gibson. The photographs on pages 17, 35, 65, by courtesy of the Most Honourable the Marquess of Bath; the photograph on page 93, by courtesy of Lord and Lady Digby. The photographs on pages 45, 97, 119, are the exclusive copyright of Mr F. Gibson, Isles of Scilly, to whom I am very grateful.

I also wish to thank the Gloucestershire and Dorset Women's Institutes for permission to quote from some of their literature.

CONTENTS

INTRODUCTION

The West Country and its people, more than in any other region of England, have been concerned with the development of marine communication, upon which so much of the economic strength of England has been built. In pre-Christian times the Phoenicians are said to have traded for tin and to have brought saffron to Cornwall, a spice still used a lot there. In the fourth and fifth centuries Irish monks founded colonies in Somerset, Devon and Cornwall, which is recorded in many place names. The leek, nettle and other herbs, together with barley, and all milk products were the mainstay of many monastic settlements, and still survive in West Country cooking.

The great seafarers of Devon and Bristol in the sixteenth, seventeenth and eighteenth centuries made certain foods such as the potato, turkeys and spices available to all, instead of the few who could afford the high prices formerly paid for them. Much of the early preservation of food was carried out by means of these spices, mincemeat having survived to the present day. The export of foods and wool from Bristol built up the vast wine trade and greatly contributed to the nation's riches, influenced the cooking of the region, and made that city famous for a sherry called 'Bristol Milk'.

In the Middle Ages much of England's wealth was founded on the Cotswold wool trade which flourished for several reasons: first, much of Europe was in a continual state of war, and secondly, the wolf had been exterminated in English forests after the Norman Conquest, whilst they still roamed in marauding packs all over the continent.

Much of the history of England has been enacted in the West Country and by West Country people. King Edgar, the first King of England (before that, England had been a heptarchy) was crowned, by Dunstan, at Bath Abbey in 973. The legend of King Alfred and the burnt cakes remains, while the battle of Athelney in which he put an end to Danish domination, is forgotten.

It was Lord Weymouth who reminded me that the West Country comprised a large part of the Anglo-Saxon Kingdom of Wessex. For that reason I have included Hampshire. Winchester was the magnificent capital of that Kingdom, and the College of St Mary, Winchester, was originated by William of Wykeham in 1387, whose educational vision included this college and New College, Oxford.

The warm climate engendered by the Gulf Stream makes much of the land in the West Country ideal for fruit and flower growing, as well as rich grazing for sheep and cattle. The apple orchards of Gloucestershire and Somerset have given us cider, and the pigs fed on the windfalls and on the nuts of the forests have produced succulent pork and ham. The world-famous Cheddar cheese, as well as Stilton and Gloucester, comes from this part of the world, and so does the incomparable Blue Vinny of Dorset which is in danger of disappearing altogether.

Many of the dishes in the following pages are familiar to me, for my maternal grandmother came from near Truro, and was brought up in Somerset: it is from her that I learnt at an early age much of the lore of the West Country, and many of the dishes herein are from her handwritten recipe book, now yellowing at the edges, but invaluable to me, for it is in everyday use. Martha Ann Cornish gave me an early love of food, and this is her book.

THEODORA FITZGIBBON 1972

Deilginis,
Baile Atha Cliath.

Dalkey,
Dublin.

From the witches
And the weasles
And the creeping things at hedge bottoms
Good Lord Deliver us.

West Country Litany.

BRAWN

The serene beauty of Gloucester cathedral dominates this ancient city, which contains the tombstone of Rufus Sita, a Roman auxiliary cavalryman from the first century A.D., and is also the burial place of Robert, Duke of Normandy (eldest son of William the Conqueror) and Edward II whose tombs are in the cathedral. The city is laid out on a cross-plan with four 'gate' streets at the main points of the compass. The remains of Blackfriars Priory are behind Southgate, and nearer to the docks are those of Llanthony Priory, built to rehouse the monks of Llanthony in the Honddu Valley when they could no longer bear with 'the Welshmen and the wolves'.

Nearby is the ancient town of Tewkesbury, whose inhabitants are reputed to have a strong, pungent wit . . . 'As thick as Tewkesbury mustard,' says Falstaff in Shakespeare's Henry IV. *It is the setting for several Victorian novels, and the Hop Pole Inn mentioned in* The Pickwick Papers *is still there. 'At the Hop Pole at Tewkesbury, they stopped to dine . . .'*

> *'Set forth mustard and brawne.'*
> *Russell,* Boke of Nurture, *1460.*

Brawn was made of any trimmings and pieces of the head of a pig that were not used to make the famous Bath Chap, which is the cheek with the tongue in it, salted and smoked. It is usually sold ready to eat in shops and is an excellent cut for a small family, either hot or cold with broad beans and parsley sauce. Brawn is like a coarse French country pâté, made from half a pickled pig's head soaked overnight, then cooked in water to cover, with fresh parsley, sage and marjoram, sliced onions, salt and plenty of peppercorns. It is cooked for about 4 hours, the stock strained off and kept, and all

Oxbody Lane (c. 1898) with Gloucester Cathedral in the background.

the bones removed from the head. The meat is cut into small pieces, and if the tongue is there it is skinned and then laid, sliced in half, between the chopped meat which has been laid carefully in the bowl it will be served from. The stock is defatted, gently warmed, then poured over the meat to cover. When cold it will be a thick jelly, and it is served cold, cut into thick slices, with mustard sauce.

MUSTARD SAUCE

2 tablespoons lard or butter
1 heaped tablespoon flour mixed with the same of dry mustard powder
½ pint (1 cup) warm milk
3 tablespoons cream

Heat the lard or butter and stir in the mixed flour and mustard and let it cook for 1 minute, then add the milk gradually, stirring all the time so that it is smooth. Simmer for about 5 minutes, then add the cream and beat it well. Let it get cold, beating just before serving and removing any skin that might have formed. This makes quite a strong sauce, but add more made mustard (well beaten in) before serving if liked very hot. Makes about ½ pint.

GLOUCESTER SAUCE

is made with mayonnaise flavoured with cayenne pepper, chopped chives, a squeeze of lemon juice and Worcestershire sauce, with a little sour cream added, all to taste, and well mixed. It is served with meat salads.

CHEESE RAMEKINS

'. . . she was come in herself for the Stilton cheese, the north Wiltshire, the butter, the cellery [sic], the beetroot, and all the dessert.' Emma, *Jane Austen, 1816. Jane Austen was one of the large number of great writers of the West Country, having been born in Steventon, Hampshire, in 1775.*

Wiltshire cheese is almost impossible to get nowadays: it is made in two varieties. The first is shaped like a double Gloucester, but the curd is heated twice, which increases the fermentation and alters the texture and flavour. The second variety is a cylindrical cheese known as 'Wiltshire loaves'. The curd is not heated twice and the taste is not unlike a Gloucester.

From a recipe of 1736

½ lb. grated double Gloucester cheese (or a mature Cheddar)
2 eggs
12 round rolls

½ lb. grated Cheshire cheese
4 tablespoons butter
pepper

Mix the two grated cheeses together, then add the butter, pepper and well-beaten eggs. Pound all together very thoroughly. Cut the rolls in half and scoop out most of the crumbs, then fill each half with the cheese mixture. Bake in a hot oven (400°F.) for about 20 minutes. They will rise over an inch, and should be eaten at once.

Serves 12.
A little finely chopped ham can be added to the cheese mixture if a more substantial snack is required.

The Cheesemarket, Salisbury, Wiltshire, c. 1870

GUINEA FOWL

This most beautiful city is a city within a city, for inside the boundaries is the ecclesiastical city, walled, containing the magnificent Cathedral, Chapter House, Deanery and Bishop's Palace, which is moated, and where the swans pull a bell when they are ready for dinner. The city is so typically England at its best that one is tempted to regard Somerset as the senior county and remember that in 973 Dunstan crowned Edgar the first King of England in Bath Abbey, Somerset.

West Country specialities such as Lardy Cake and Somerset fritters (which are large currant-studded pancakes cooked in the oven), Catherine (Cattern) cakes (see page 110) are all to be found, with many others, in the nearby Old Priory Café, hot from the oven.

Guinea Fowl, known as 'Gliny' in the West Country, is not unlike a pheasant, in that it can be dry if plainly roasted. The following recipe is good for both birds. Gliny can also be cooked as Rock Cornish hen.

THE STUFFING for 1 large bird
½ lb. sausage meat
the liver of the bird, chopped
a pinch of mixed spice and nutmeg
2 small chopped mushrooms
salt and pepper
1 guinea fowl and giblets, boiled

4 bacon rashers
3 tablespoons oil
*1 glass port (about 6 tablespoons)
1 cup giblet stock
3 tablespoons cream (optional)
*Cider can be used instead of port if liked.

Mix all the stuffing ingredients together and put them into the body of the bird. (The sausage meat gives the bird an inner baste of fat.) Put into the roasting tin and cover the breast with the rashers of bacon, pour over the oil, and roast in a moderate oven (350°F.) for 20 minutes. Take out, and add the giblet stock and port or cider, then put back and continue roasting for a further 35 minutes, basting from time to time. When ready, remove the bird to a warmed dish, and boil up the pan juices on top of the stove. Taste for seasoning, and add a very little more port and stock mixed, if it has reduced too much. Just before serving stir in the cream, if using, and heat up, but do not reboil. Serve redcurrant jelly separately.

Enough for about 3 – 4 depending on the size of the bird.

The Market Place, Wells, Somerset, with the Cathedral in background, c. 1890

CLIFTON PUFFS

Isambard Brunel's famous suspension bridge was begun in 1832 and finished in 1864. Clifton has famous hot springs which issue from an aperture at the foot of St Vincent's Rock in the area known as Hotwells. The water has a temperature of about 76°F, and a hydropathic establishment is situated nearby.

'... I inquired [sic] if that little town could consume such a quantity of veal; (it was market-day) they told me the boats were ready in the river to buy for Bristol. And this was doubtless the case with butter etc.' A Six Weeks' Tour through the Southern Counties and Wales, Arthur Young, 1768.

A traditional small cake which is rich yet light

FOR THE PASTRY
10 oz. (2½ cups) flour
2 oz. (½ cup) ground rice
4 oz. (1 cup) ground almonds
1 lb. (2 cups) butter
a squeeze of lemon juice
a pinch of salt
6 tablespoons iced water
1 egg and sugar to garnish

FOR THE FILLING
½ lb. peeled, cored & finely
   chopped eating apples
½ lb. (1 cup) currants
¼ lb. (½ cup) seedless raisins
1 cup chopped candied peel
2 cups blanched, chopped
   almonds
½ teaspoon grated nutmeg
4-6 tablespoons brandy

First make the puff pastry, and see that all ingredients are cold except the butter, which should be soft but not oily and still in a block. Rub 2 tablespoons butter into the flour which has been well mixed with the salt, ground rice and almonds, then add the water and lemon juice and mix to a firm dough. Roll out to a rectangle about ½ in. thick, and put the whole of the remaining slab of butter into the middle. Fold over, press the edges down well and leave to stand for 15 minutes. With the sealed edges facing away from the cook, roll out the pastry, outwards, until it is three times the size. Then fold it into three, turn the open edge to face the cook and roll again. Leave to rest as before, and repeat the folding into three, rolling and resting twice more so that in all the pastry has been rolled and rested 6 times. If it still looks fat-streaked give it an extra turn. Wrap and chill before use.

Meanwhile, mix all the filling ingredients well, cover, and leave in a warm place to infuse for about 1 hour. Then roll out the pastry very thinly and cut into 4-in. squares. Put some of the mixture on one half of each square, damp the edges, and fold over cornerwise, making triangles. Brush with beaten egg, dust with coarsely crushed sugar and bake in a hot oven (400°F.) for about 15-20 minutes, or until the pastry is risen and a pale gold. They are excellent served warm.

Makes about 20.

Clifton Suspension Bridge and a paddle steamer, c. 1880

ROAST SADDLE OF LAMB WITH PLUM SAUCE

The origin of 'giants' is obscure, and the West Country seems to abound in them (see page 92). This one was first recorded in 1496 and is supposed to represent St Christopher and the Hob Nob or Dragon. Formerly, it was used in the Midsummer pageants of the Merchant Tailors; for all important markets, fairs and merrymaking. It was paraded for exceptional occasions such as the 1832 Reform Bill; the festival for the peace after the Crimean War, and Queen Victoria's Diamond Jubilee in 1897. The Giant came out for the peace after the second world war, and its latest appearance was for the Coronation of Elizabeth II in 1953.

The following poster was put up at the cessation of the Crimean War, 29th May, 1856, for the celebrations with the Giant:
   'Morrice [sic] Dancers, Trumpeters, Bands,
   Roasted sheep, Dinner at 1 o'clock
   Afterwards:
   Rural sports and Old English Games in the Green Croft,
   Grand Display of Fireworks in the Market Place at 9 o'clock.'

Salisbury Plain was famous for the wild Great Bustard which weighs up to 14 pounds. It was always served for the inaugural banquets for the Mayor of Salisbury, the last recorded banquet it was served at being in 1871. However, this giant bird has now been re-introduced under protected conditions.
   '. . . because sheep is one of the great things here, and sheep in a country like this must be kept in flocks to be any profit.'
   William Cobbett, 1766-1835.

Plum sauce with lamb or mutton is an old Wiltshire method and very good it is.

A saddle is the classic joint of lamb or mutton. It is the two loins together from ribs to tail, and can weigh up to 10 pounds. The kidneys are sometimes attached to the saddle, sometimes they are removed and tucked into the bone on top. They can be cooked with the joint, but for my taste this overcooks them, and I prefer to cook them separately and put them back before serving. Dust the joint with black pepper, add a sprig of rosemary inside, and cover with a little oil or dripping. Roast in a moderate oven (350°F.) for 20 minutes to the pound, and when ready drain off all excess fat and add a large glass of port or red wine to the pan juices. Season well and reduce on top of the stove until it thickens slightly. Serve with redcurrant jelly. The saddle should be carved along the backbone as you would carve a duck.

PLUM SAUCE

Stew one pound of stoned plums gently in ½ pint of white wine vinegar with 4 oz. sugar, for about 10 minutes or until soft. When ready stir in a tablespoon chopped fresh mint. Serve hot.

'The Giant' crossing Blue Boar Row, Salisbury, Wiltshire, 1897

CLOTTED CREAM AND SYLLABUB

'. . . My landlady brought me one of the West Country tarts . . . it is an apple pie with a custard all on the top. It is the most acceptable entertainment that could be made me. They scald their cream and milk in most parts of these counties, and so it is a sort of clouted cream as we call it, with a little sugar, and so put on the top of the apple pie.'
Through England on a Side-Saddle, Celia Fiennes, 1662-1741.

CLOTTED CREAM

Set very fresh milk to stand in a wide earthenware pan with handles, for 12 hours in summer or 24 hours in winter. Then heat slowly, never allowing it to boil, until the shape of the bottom of the pan is outlined in the cream as a circle concentric to the rim. Without shaking the pan, remove from the heat and leave to cool for a further 12 hours in a cool place. The thick crust of cream is then skimmed off with a large spoon or a slice. The top will be a golden yellow and very creamy underneath. This cream is used in many ways in both Devon and Cornwall: spread on little buns, called splits; poured into pork and leek pies; and in 'Lammy pie', which is lamb layered with a lot of chopped parsley and cream, with pastry over the top.

SYLLABUB

The name comes from 'sille' the wine from a part of the Champagne district, and 'bub' which was Elizabethan slang for a sparkling drink.

1 pint (2 cups) heavy cream	2 lemons
4 tablespoons sherry	4 oz. (1 cup) caster
4 tablespoons brandy	(extrafine) sugar
a sprig of rosemary	a pinch of nutmeg

Grate the peel of the lemons very finely, then squeeze out the juice. Mix together with the sherry and brandy, the nutmeg, sugar and rosemary, then leave to stand for several hours or overnight. Strain, and half fill some tall glasses with the liquid. Whip the cream well and pour over the top. Fruit juice or a thin purée of such fruits as raspberries or redcurrant can be used instead of lemon. Leave to get quite cold.

Serves 6-8.

In the last century, cider was often used instead of the sherry, but a drop of brandy is essential to the taste. Some cooks whip the fruit liquid and the whipped cream together, but I prefer the refreshing fruit and wine at the bottom.

Making clotted cream, East Ogwell, Devon, c. 1900

LAMPREYS

Gloucester is the most inland port in England, and the docks are situated where the Gloucester Sharpness Canal is connected with the River Severn. The original Old Dock was opened in 1827, other docks being added in 1849 and 1892. The Bore is the name of the Severn's tidal wave which happens from time to time and carries considerable force. Lampreys and elvers (see page 98) are still traditional fare on Severnside.

'Lampreys are one of my passions.' Elizabeth I of England.

A particularly brave statement considering that one of her ancestors, Henry I of England, is said to have died from a 'surfeit of lampreys'.

Lampreys are a curious eel-like fish with a cartilaginous skeleton, no bones, no limbs and no jaws. They can reach about a yard in length and are still caught in the Severn Estuary. Lamperns are much smaller, live in rivers, and are thought by many to be the greater delicacy. Until 1836 the City of Gloucester sent a huge lamprey pie to the reigning monarch every year.

'Of this kind of fish there are two different sorts in general use for the table, one being the sea or marine lamprey, which is abundant at Gloucester and Worcester, where it is dressed and preserved for the purpose of being given as presents'. Francatelli, 1886 (Chief Cook-in-Ordinary to Queen Victoria).

To prepare lampreys, scald them in boiling water before skinning; two small filaments in the back should be removed as they are thought to be poisonous. They may be cooked in any way as for eels, but the following recipe by William Augustus Henderson, 1797, is of interest.

'Having skinned, gutted and thoroughly washed your fish, season them with salt, pepper, a little lemon-peel shred fine, mace, cloves and nutmeg. Put some thin slices of butter into your stewpan and having rolled your fish round, put them in, with half a pint of good gravy, a gill of white wine, a bunch of marjoram, winter savory, thyme, and an onion sliced. Let them stew over a gentle fire, and keep turning them till they are tender. Then take them out, and put an anchovy to the sauce. Thicken it with the yolk of an egg beat very fine, or a piece of butter rolled in flour . . . pour it over the fish and serve them to table.'

I have enjoyed them immensely cooked similarly to the above, but using red wine, with a mirepoix of carrots, onions, shallots, bayleaf, and served with young leeks, chopped and softened in olive oil.

HAM COOKED WITH CIDER, AND DAMSON SAUCE

'Every well-found house should make it a point of honour to keep a good ham in cut . . . I know of no better accompaniment . . . than . . . damsons pickled in the following way.' Arthur Quiller-Couch ('Q', the author).

4-5 lb. ham
2 pints (4 cups) cider
1 large onion stuck with cloves
1 tablespoon brown sugar
½ lemon

a sprig each of parsley and marjoram
pepper
4 heaped tablespoons of brown sugar mixed with ½ teaspoon mace and 3 heaped tablespoons crisp breadcrumbs

Soak the ham overnight, then scrape the skin, and pat it fairly dry. Put into a large saucepan with enough cider barely to cover, add the onion, 1 tablespoon brown sugar, herbs, pepper and the half lemon. Bring to the boil, then let it simmer gently for 25 minutes to the pound. Let it cool in the stock, then peel off the skin. Now mix together the remaining brown sugar, mace and breadcrumbs which have been just moistened with a very little defatted stock. Press this mixture over the fatty part of the ham and put the joint into a baking tin with about 1 cup cider stock. (If the pan is lined with foil it will prevent the bottom becoming sticky.) Bake in a moderate oven for 40 minutes, when the gravy should be an aromatic, sticky mixture.

'Q's' PICKLED DAMSONS

(Should be made at least one week in advance)
6 lb. damsons
3 lb. lump sugar
1½ pints (3 cups) white wine vinegar or cider vinegar

½ oz. stick cinnamon
1 teaspoon cloves (in a muslin bag)

First remove the stones from the damsons, taking care to reserve the juice. Pour the vinegar over the fruit and leave overnight: strain off the juice, boil up, pour over the fruit and leave till next day. Repeat this once more, then boil all the ingredients together for about 20-30 minutes. Remove the spices and put the pickled damsons into sterilised warmed jars and make airtight. This can be served cold, or with the chill just off, if the ham is warm.

Makes about 6 lb.

Plums can also be used.

*Open-air Feast to celebrate Queen
Victoria's Diamond Jubilee,
Kingsbridge, Devon, 1897*

CHICKEN AND HAM PASTE

The New Forest is over a hundred square miles in size and has some of the finest oak and beech trees in Britain. Semi-wild ponies roam at will, and the Hampshire hog is turned out to free-range for the beechnuts and acorns during the pannage months. Hog pudding (a kind of boiled sausage) used to be traditional Hampshire fare, but seldom seen nowadays. However, the local streams still have abundant crayfish, that most delicate freshwater prawn, and watercress beds abound. At Christchurch, saltwater salmon are a local delicacy. Grapes are grown near Hambleden and Beaulieu and extremely good table wine is still made and sold there. Winchester, the ancient Saxon capital of Wessex, is also thought by some to be Camelot, of Arthurian romance.

'Sir Balin's sword was put into marble stone, standing as upright as a great millstone, and it swam down the stream to the city of Camelot – that is, in English, Winchester.'

History of Prince Arthur.

1 lightly boiled, boned chicken, about 3 pounds
½ lb. chicken livers
1 lb. ham
1 tablespoon chopped parsley
salt and pepper

melted butter
1 chopped shallot
2 heaped tablespoons·butter
½ pint (1 cup) chicken stock
a pinch each of ground cloves and allspice

Leftover chicken can also be used, but in that case increase the amount of ham and liver.

Cut the liver and ham in small pieces. Melt 2 tablespoons of butter in a pan and lightly fry the shallot, then the liver and ham and finally the parsley. Stir it frequently and season to taste. Pour off the fat and either mash or liquidise the liver. Cut the chicken into thin slices, season, and sprinkle with the spices. In a deep greased dish put a layer of liver, then chicken, then ham and shallot, and so on until the dish is full, ending with the liver. Pour the stock over, cover, and either steam, or bake in a tin of hot water to half-way up the dish, for 2 hours. When cooked, press it down with a spoon, and when cold, cover it with melted butter, and chill. Serve cold, cut into slices, either as a first course or as a light meal with salad. It also makes excellent picnic fare, for it is like a delicate *terrine*.

Serves about 8.

Picnic in the New Forest, Hampshire, 1886

SALLY LUNN CAKES

Was there a pretty, buxom, West Country lass called Sally Lunn who sold hot, golden cakes in the streets of Bath in the eighteenth century? Many people in Bath think so, and point to her house and shop in Lilliput Alley. It is undoubtedly true that such a girl 'cried' these cakes, but what she called was West Country French, 'Solet Lune', (Sun and Moon) which is descriptive of a golden-topped cake.

1½ lb. (6 cups) flour	4 oz. (½ cup) butter
a pinch of salt	1 pint (2 cups) tepid milk
1 oz. yeast creamed with 2 tablespoons sugar	3 eggs

Mix the flour and salt in a basin, then beat the yeast to a cream with the sugar. Soften the butter in the lukewarm milk and add the yeast. (If the milk is too hot it will kill the yeast.) Pour this gradually into the centre of the flour, and add 2 of the eggs, well beaten. Mix all well, and knead lightly until a stiff dough is formed. Cover with a cloth and leave to rise in a warm place for about 2 hours, then knead again lightly until quite smooth. Shape into about 8 cakes and either put them into round greased baking rings or small tins. Separate the white from the yolk of the remaining egg and brush the tops over with the beaten egg-yolk, then bake in a hot oven (400°F.) for about 20 minutes, or until firm when pressed and a golden brown. Slip off the rings, or take from the tin, split open, filling the middle with whipped cream which has been mixed with the stiffly beaten egg-white, slightly sweetened to taste. They should be eaten just warm.

DAMASK CREAM

A Bath junket, *par excellence*

1 pint (2 cups) light cream	1 teaspoon rennet or junket tablets
2 heaped tablespoons caster (extrafine) sugar	3 teaspoons rosewater
a pinch of mace or nutmeg	4 tablespoons cream
deep red rose petals	1 tablespoon fine sugar

Make the junket in the usual way, by bringing the pint of cream, caster sugar and 2 teaspoons rosewater to blood heat, then dissolving the tablet, or stirring in the rennet.

Set in the dish it will be served from, sprinkle with mace or nutmeg and leave to set. Just before serving pour over the 4 tablespoons cream mixed with 1 teaspoon of rosewater and the fine sugar. Serve surrounded by the red rose petals.

In Devon and Cornwall it is served with a layer of clotted cream on top.

Enough for 4.

Sally Lunn's shop and house, Lilliput
Alley, Bath, Somerset, c. 1880

SAFFRON CAKE

St Ives was founded by an Irish saint, I'a, in the fifth century, and although it is nowadays well known for its colony of artists, it has always been remarkable for its fish, particularly pilchards, many of which are exported to Italy and other Mediterranean countries. As many as 75 million have been netted in a single day. '. . . The fish taken about St Ives are salmon-peal, ling, codfish, mullet, bass, hake, bream, and whiting, plaice, soles, turbot in plenty, as also gurnards red and grey, mackerel but not many, herrings, pilchards, and for this fish it is the best place in Cornwall; of these have been taken 1,500 barrels in a day, some say 1,800. Here also are taken lobsters, crabs which they call pollacks . . . dogfish, dranicks (as they call them) tomlins . . . which are nothing but a young codfish, shads . . . dories . . . sandeels, lauces . . .'
                                                    John Ray, 1627-1705.

'All along the cliffs, as we rode upon the sand towards St. Ives, grew Foeniculum vulgare (fennel) in great plenty.' ibid.

As well as fennel, which is excellent for putting with grilled fish, or in a fish soup, Cornwall is also noted for its use of saffron. It is believed to have been introduced into Cornwall by the Phoenicians when they came to trade for tin, but it was also used in many other parts of England, and was grown extensively at Saffron Walden, Essex (walde, the Anglo-Saxon for 'field') and at Hinton in Cambridgeshire, the people growing them being known as 'crokers' as the spice comes from the purple saffron crocus (Crocus sativus). It has, however, survived longer in Cornwall than anywhere else in England and saffron cakes are still a daily, and delicious, feature of Cornish life.

These quantities make 3 large loaves (8-in. tin), so reduce if less is needed.

2 lb. (8 cups) plain flour	1 lb. (2 cups) currants
$\frac{1}{2}$ teaspoon saffron covered with 3 tablespoons boiling water and left to soak for 8 hours	2 oz. ($\frac{1}{2}$ cup) chopped candied peel
1 oz. yeast dissolved in $1\frac{1}{4}$ pints ($2\frac{1}{2}$ cups) tepid water and a pinch of sugar	8 oz. (1 cup) granulated sugar
	1 lb. (2 cups) butter or margarine
	pinch of salt

First soak the saffron overnight in the water. The next day sponge the yeast in the tepid water and sugar and a cup of flour, mix well together and stand in a warm place to rise. Rub the butter into the remaining flour, add the salt and sugar, mixing well, then add the fruit and peel. Pour the yeast mixture into a well in the centre of the flour mixture and add the saffron and water, slightly warmed. Mix very well into a soft dough. Cover and put in a warm place to rise until it has doubled in size, then knead and punch the dough down until any air bubbles have gone. Put into greased tins, and let rise a little, then bake for about 1-$1\frac{1}{4}$ hours at $330°F$. Turn out when cool. This mixture can also be shaped into little buns, and baked for not more than $\frac{1}{2}$ hour.

20

Porthminster Beach, St Ives, Cornwall, c. 1912

DEVILLED BONES

'Bumping the Bounds' was a curious and arduous ceremony to show the young generation the boundaries, which took place in Bristol. The last time it was done was 1900 and the following abridged account gives an idea of the elaborate and exhausting proceedings which it entailed.

'The perambulation of the city boundaries, considered to be essential . . . was commenced on September 10th when about one hundred gentlemen, members and officers of the Corporation met near the bottom of St. Vincent's Rocks, where three hundred policemen with trumpeters and banner bearers already assembled. . . . On reaching Purdown after a five miles march, they halted for luncheon. The day's perambulation finished at the Frenchay road where tea was provided . . . The proceedings were resumed on the 12th . . . and a halt was called at Magpie Bottom. On the 13th the perambulation was resumed at the same spot, much of the day's journey being over somewhat difficult country, interspaced with water-cress beds, marshes, orchards and gardens. The Avon was reached near Conham, whence two steam vessels conveyed the visitors to Hanham Weir, the eastern extremity of the river jurisdiction. Luncheon was provided at Hanham Court, and after a brief rest the company returned to Conham by water, climbed the steep bank on the Somerset shore and made for St. Anne's Park and Brislington . . .'

This sauce is very good for meaty leftovers on the bone, spare-ribs, joints of poultry or game, or for serving with grilled or boiled chops.

4 heaped tablespoons butter	1 teaspoon French mustard
1 heaped tablespoon flour	1 tablespoon soft chutney
1 teaspoon dry mustard	1 tablespoon Worcestershire
1 cup gravy or stock	sauce

If using poultry remove the skin from the poultry joints, and if using meat remove any gristle. For the sauce, mash the butter on a plate, then well work into it the flour; add the dry mustard to form a paste. Now add the French mustard, the chutney and the Worcestershire sauce. See that the paste is fairly firm; if it is too thin work in a little more flour, so that it is easily spreadable. Cover the joints all over with this, and then grill them under a medium flame. For a sauce to pour around, heat the gravy or stock, and add a knob of the devil mixture into it. See that the flour is well cooked, and stir while heating the sauce. Pour it round the devilled joints and serve. Without using the gravy this is also an excellent way to serve grilled kidneys: spread the sauce over just before sending to table.

Serves 4-6.

CRAB

Devon is famous for excellent fish: Brixham is an active fishing port which brings in mackerel, soles, turbot, dories, squid, crab and lobster. The rivers produce good salmon, which is served on local menus under the river names: Torridge, Exe, Taw, and so on. It is often poached in the vin du pays, *cider, with fresh herbs, and thickened with butter rolled in flour, before adding some good Devonshire cream. Crab is perhaps the most traditional shellfish of Devon and Cornwall, with mackerel and the sometimes elusive pilchard making a superb meal when caught and cooked the same day.*

BUTTERED CRAB

2 good-sized crabs (or equivalent canned)
2 anchovy fillets
½ pint (1 cup) white wine
a pinch of grated nutmeg
1 cup white breadcrumbs
salt and pepper
3 tablespoons butter
slices of buttered toast

Mash the anchovy fillets in the wine, add the nutmeg and the breadcrumbs. Season to taste. Bring gently to the boil and simmer for 5 minutes. Mix the flaked crabmeat with the butter and add to the hot wine mixture. Cook for 4 minutes and serve with the toast cut, and placed around the dish.

Serves 4-6.

If the breadcrumbs and wine are omitted, and the other ingredients are thoroughly mashed, this can be potted and preserved by covering the top, when cold, with melted butter. It will keep for several weeks in a cold place, so long as the top is sealed.

DEVIL SAUCE FOR CRAB
(enough for 2 large crabs)

¼ pint (½ cup) thick cream
1 teaspoon anchovy paste
¼ teaspoon dry mustard
1 tablespoon Worcestershire sauce
1 tablespoon mushroom ketchup
salt, pepper and a dash of cayenne

Whip the cream until thick, and gradually add the other ingredients, whisking to keep the sauce thick. Put the crabmeat into an oven-proof dish, spread the devil on top and either grill under a medium grill, or bake in a hot oven for 5-10 minutes. Serve with wedges of lemon.

Seine Fishing in Devon, c. 1900

LAMB ROASTED AND STUFFED WITH APPLES AND CIDER

This Regency Spa came into prominence when George III came to recuperate there, although it was a Saxon and medieval village long before that. Much of the opulence and wealth of the 'Queen of the Cotswolds' is based on the wool trade which in 1297 amounted to half the value of the whole land. In England, the wolf was exterminated after the Conquest, whereas it existed until the seventeenth century in many continental forests, thus making sheep farming difficult. The coarse texture of the Cotswold wool was ideally suited to making the famous West of England cloth, and it is understandable that a wealthy wool merchant engraved the following on the windows of his large new house in the sixteenth century:

> *'I praise God and ever shall*
> *It is the sheep hath paid for it all.'*

5 lb. boned loin of lamb	2 teaspoons ginger
juice and peel of 1 lemon	salt and pepper
1 lb. cooking apples peeled and and cored	2 tablespoons dripping, or oil
2 tablespoons sugar	2 cups cider or apple juice
3 cloves	

Rub the lamb inside and out with the lemon juice and peel, then lay slices of apple inside the meat, sprinkle with sugar, dot with the cloves and roll up, skewering or sewing up firmly. Rub the outside with a mixture of the ginger, salt and pepper and brush over with oil. Put into a baking pan and roast in a moderate oven for 20 minutes to the pound. Warm up the cider and baste with the warm juice every 20 minutes. Drain off any excess fat when it is cooked, reduce the gravy on a hot flame until it is about half, and serve it separately in a gravy boat.

Serves 8.

Cheltenham is also well known for its sausages, crumpets and cakes. A suet pudding made with fruit including crystallized ginger was formerly made, and served with brandy sauce. I can, however, find no recipe for it.

CHELTENHAM CAKES

2 lb. flour	1 pint (2 cups) warm milk
¼ lb. (½ cup) butter	2 egg-yolks
1 oz. yeast creamed with teaspoon sugar	

Melt the butter in milk and add all ingredients except yeast and mix well. Then add the yeast which has been creamed with a teaspoon sugar. Cover and set to rise for 2 hours. Shape into small buns, and let rise again, then bake in a sharp oven (400°F.) for 15 minutes. Serve warm with butter.

Makes about 20.

At the Winter Gardens, Cheltenham Promenade, Gloucestershire, c. 1872. Photographer,
Domenico Barnett, 1839-1911, music teacher at Cheltenham Ladies College, 1867-1911

DEVON PORK PIE

'*The squab pye, the herb pye, the leek and pork pye, on which clouted cream was profusely poured – the goose and parsnip, and the fish and apple pye were frequent . . .*' Richard Polwhele, *1760-1838*.

Traditions and Recollections, *1816*.

Devon Pork Pie is also called Dartmouth pie: if made with lamb or veal it is called locally Squab pie.

6 pork loin chops, boned	a pinch of nutmeg and
3 medium peeled and sliced	a pinch of allspice
onions, or 6 medium sized	2 tablespoons sugar
leeks, chopped	1 pint (2 cups) stock, or cider,
6 medium, peeled, cored and	or white wine
sliced apples	salt and pepper
	8 oz. shortcrust pastry (see page 54)

Trim the chops and cut in half if very large. Put half the amount in the bottom of a deep pie-dish, then a layer of sliced apple, a sprinkle of the spices and the sugar and then follow with the onions and salt and pepper. Repeat this, then add the stock, cider or wine. Moisten the edges of the pie dish with water, then put on the pastry lid, pressing the edges down very well. Brush over with a little milk, put into a moderate oven (375°F.) for 15 minutes, then cover the pastry with foil, reduce the heat to about 300°F. and continue cooking for a further $1\frac{1}{4}$ hours. Pour over a little warmed cream when serving, if liked, but it makes the pie very rich.

Serves 6.

Open fireplace at Wingstone-Manaton Farm, Devon, for many years the home of John Galsworthy, c. 1900.

BAKED MACKEREL WITH RHUBARB

'Once upon a time there was a little chimney-sweep, and his name was Tom . . . He cried when he had to climb the dark flues, rubbing his poor knees and elbows raw; and when the soot got into his eyes, which it did every day in the week; and when his master beat him, which he did every day of the week . . . And he laughed the other half of the day, when he was tossing halfpennies with the other boys, or playing leap-frog over the posts . . . and he thought of the fine times coming, when he would be a man, and a master-sweep . . .' Charles Kingsley, The Water Babies. Kingsley was himself a West Country man, having been born at Bideford, Devon, in 1819.

'But as the pavements of Bristol are not the widest or cleanest upon earth, so its streets are not altogether the straightest or least intricate; and Mr. Winkle being greatly puzzled by their manifold windings and twistings, looked about him for a decent shop in which he could apply afresh for counsel and instruction.' The Pickwick Papers, by Charles Dickens (who was born in Portsmouth).

Baked Mackerel with Rhubarb is a speciality of Bristol and the West Country.

8 cleaned and filleted mackerel	FOR THE SAUCE
8 bayleaves	1 lb. chopped rhubarb
24 whole black peppercorns	8 tablespoons cider
salt	a squeeze of lemon
6 tablespoons cider	4 tablespoons brown sugar
1 heaped tablespoon butter	$\frac{1}{2}$ teaspoon mace or nutmeg

Lay the filleted fish out and on each one lay a bayleaf, several peppercorns and a little salt. Roll them up and put side by side in an ovenproof dish, pour over the cider and dot with butter. Cover with foil or a lid, and bake in a moderate oven (350°F.) for about $\frac{1}{2}$ hour. Meanwhile cook together all the sauce ingredients over a low flame until it is quite soft and like a purée: it should be fairly dry. If liked it can be sieved, but is quite acceptable as it is. Serve separately, hot, with the mackerel.

Serves 4.

Boy chimney-sweeps in Steep Street,
Bristol, 1870

SPEECH HOUSE PUDDING

The miniature Forest of Dean, created 'Royal' in Saxon times, and once famous for iron and coal, is now mainly common land, the pasture for cattle, sheep, pigs and ponies. Speech House (now an hotel) was built in Charles II's reign as the Verderers and Freeminers Court, to settle disputes amongst the foresters and miners. The Verderers' court-room with its large fireplace where joints once turned on the spit is still there. Speech House Pudding was the traditional speciality.

4 oz. (½ cup) soft butter
4 separated eggs
2 oz. (¼ cup) caster sugar
4 oz. (1 cup) plain flour

½ lb. raspberry jam
1 teaspoon bicarbonate of soda
    dissolved in 2 tablespoons
    milk

Grease a 1½-pint pudding basin or mould with a little of the butter and then in another basin cream together the butter and sugar. Beat in the beaten egg yolks one at a time, then add the flour, a spoonful at a time, beating well after each addition. Mix in 2 tablespoons of the jam. Beat the egg whites until stiff. Mix the bicarbonate of soda into the milk, add to the mixture then quickly fold in the egg whites. Fill the basin three-quarters full, cover with foil and either boil in a saucepan with boiling water just up to the rim for 2½ hours, or steam in a steamer for 3 hours. If boiling, be sure not to let the water run dry, adding more boiling water if needed. Turn out by inverting a warm plate over the basin and tipping it quickly over, and serve with the rest of the jam which has been heated, poured over the top. Cream can be served if liked, but it is not essential.

Serves 4-6.

EGGS WITH LETTUCE

Longleat House, the residence of the Marquess of Bath and Viscount Weymouth, is one of the finest Elizabethan houses in Britain. The grounds were landscaped by Capability Brown in the eighteenth century. It is open daily to the public.

Eggs with Lettuce, from an old manuscript receipt book, dated 1776: 'Scald some cabbage lettuce in fair water, squeeze them well, then slice them and toss them up in a saucepan with a piece of butter; season them with pepper, salt and a little nutmeg. Let them stew gently for half-an-hour, then chop them well together. When they are enough, lay them on your (warmed) dish, and keep warm. Fry some eggs nicely in butter, and lay on them. Garnish with slices of Sevile [*sic*] orange.'

This old recipe is a good one for using lettuce which is inclined to bolt and seed. Spinach may also be used if wished. About one pound of lettuce or spinach is needed for 2 servings.

ELDERFLOWER CHAMPAGNE

Home made wines are a feature of Wiltshire life. Lord Alexander Weymouth has many varieties at Longleat House and a special Chateau Longleat Wine Label has been designed as an added attraction.

This one is extremely simple to make and can be drunk in 3 weeks, but if left for about 2 months it improves enormously.

6 heads of freshly picked elderflowers in full bloom
1 gallon of cold water
$1\frac{1}{2}$ lb. sugar
2 tablespoons white wine vinegar
the juice and rind of 1 lemon

Squeeze the juice of the lemon, then cut the rind into quarters and put this with the elderflowers in a large basin. Add the sugar and vinegar, then pour over the cold water and stir well so that the sugar dissolves. Cover, and leave to steep in a cool place for 24 hours, then strain off and bottle in screw-topped bottles. It foams delightfully when poured. Makes about $1\frac{1}{4}$ gallons.

Young riders at Longleat House, Warminster, Wiltshire, August 1872

RAW TATTIE FRY

Known as Potato Jowdle when the bacon is omitted. It is a very popular breakfast or supper dish, particularly with children, especially if a fried egg is served on top.

6 slices streaky bacon
1 large sliced onion
salt and pepper

4 large potatoes, thinly sliced
approximately ½ pint (1 cup) water

Fry the bacon lightly, and when the fat begins to run out add the thinly sliced onion and fry gently for about 4 minutes, turning the onion over from time to time. Then add the thinly sliced potatoes, season to taste, and pour over the water, to about ¼ inch of the top. Put a lid on and simmer gently until the potatoes are soft which, depending on the variety, should be about ½ hour. Leave the top off for a few minutes before they are ready, to crisp up. Raw Fry is best made in a large frying pan or skillet.

Serves 2-4.

DEVON POT CAKE

12 oz. (3 cups) flour
4 oz. (½ cup) butter or margarine
2 oz. (¼ cup) lard

4 oz. (1 cup) each sultanas and currants
1 egg
1 cup milk
a pinch of salt

Blackcurrants, gooseberries or apples can be used instead of the dried fruit.

Mix together the egg and the milk, beating well. Mix the flour, butter, lard and salt together until it is like pastry. Then add the egg and milk mixing very thoroughly, and finally stir in the fruit. Roll out on a floured table, to the size of a large frying pan, grease the pan and put in the mixture. Then cook slowly, either on top of the stove, browning well on both sides, or in a moderate oven (325°F.) for about 1 hour. When ready, split open, spread with butter and brown sugar.

Frying breakfast at the circus, Devon, c. 1900

BLACKMORE VALE CAKE

This has been the cake of the Blackmore Vale Hunt for over one hundred years.

¼ lb. (½ cup) butter
¼ lb. (½ cup) caster
  (extrafine) sugar
¼ pint (½ cup) warm milk
2 teaspoons treacle (molasses)
  or golden syrup

1 teaspoon bicarbonate of soda
¾ lb. (3 cups) flour
¾ lb. (1½ cups) seedless raisins
3 oz. (1 cup) mixed chopped
  candied peel

Cream the butter and sugar until light and fluffy. Warm the milk to blood heat and add the treacle and bicarbonate of soda and let them dissolve. Add the flour gradually to the creamed butter, moistening with the milk mixture and beating well after each addition. Mix in the raisins and peel. Put into a lined and greased tin about 6 inches across and bake below the middle, in a moderate (350°F.) oven for 2½ hours.

Old Forge, Dorset, 1889

IDER

'Cider in a word is the most wholesome drink in Europe as specially sovereign against the scorbute, the stone, spleen and whatnot.' Pomona, *John Evelyn, 1729.*

    Cider, also known as 'Scrumpie' in the West Country, is made from fermented apple juice. The word comes through the Greek, from the Hebrew word, shekar, *meaning strong drink. Certainly anyone who has drunk deeply into 'Scrumpie' will remember the strong drink part. It can be used in many ways, as it is in Normandy, where it forms a part of the many famous* à la Normande *dishes. As a marinade for meats, poultry or game, it is excellent, and it can be used in place of white wine, although it imparts a different flavour. There are many recipes throughout the book using cider as the cooking liquid.*

To make cider can be chancy without a cider press, but I have used the following recipe with good results.

8 lb. apples	3 large juicy lemons
2 gallons boiling water	piece of bruised ginger root
8 lb. sugar (approx.)	

Do not use metal spoons for stirring or squeezing. Put the unpeeled apples into a large, preferably wooden, container, crush them well, pour over the boiling water, cover with a cloth and leave for a fortnight, squeezing the apples against the side daily. Strain, add the ginger and measure the juice, allowing $\frac{1}{2}$ lb. sugar to each pint of liquor. Add the lemon juice and stir well until the sugar has dissolved. Add a teacup of boiling water to raise the temperature, cover, and leave to stand for about 14 days or until a scum has formed on the surface. When this happens all over, skim it off thoroughly and pour into screw-top bottles, screwing down loosely for 2 days, then tightening them fully. Store in a cool, dry, and dark place. Do not move or shake them for at least 2 months, preferably 3.

CIDER PUNCH

Combine 2 quarts of cider with $\frac{1}{2}$ bottle of gin or vodka and $\frac{1}{4}$ bottle of sherry. Wash and slice 2 unpeeled oranges and 1 lemon, then add to the cider mixture with 3 tablespoons sugar. Crush about 3 sprigs of fresh mint and add, then chill well. Just before serving add 1 cold syphon soda, or more if it is too strong for your taste. Serve with ice, or chilled.

Makes about 20 drinks.

Cider Press, Ipplepen, Devon, c. 1898

SLOE GIN

Flint-knapping, that is making flints for guns and tinder boxes, was formerly a Wiltshire craft due to the prevalence of flint. The whole country is rich in Neolithic barrows and tombs complete with flint axe-heads. Flint Jack was a great rogue who was quick to realize the financial possibilities available: he fabricated many 'Neolithic' flints himself and became quite a well-known character in so doing.

Damsons, or small unripe plums, especially the wild variety, called bullace, can be used instead of sloes. Black cherries are good done the same way with either brandy or gin.

Sloes   White sugar
Gin

Wash and prick the sloes (a large darning needle is a good implement), then mix them with an equal amount of sugar. Half fill the bottles with this and top up with gin. Cork them tightly. It is ready to drink in 2-3 months, but the longer it is kept the better. Sloe gin is a delicious drink and very potent. If using black cherries, keep the soaked cherries afterwards for a super-de-luxe fruit salad.

PICKLED EGGS

They are a West Country speciality and are found in many pubs in the vicinity. For home use they are excellent for an *hors d'oeuvre*, or as a snack with cheese or cold meat.

16 hard-boiled eggs (boiled for 10 minutes)
½ oz. black peppercorns
½ oz. allspice
½ oz. piece of stem ginger

1 quart white vinegar (wine vinegar, and especially tarragon vinegar, gives a more delicate flavour)

Remove the egg shells and put the eggs into wide-necked jars. Boil the spices with the vinegar and whilst hot pour it over the eggs. When cold, cover tightly, and store in a cool dry place. They are ready to eat in about 2 weeks, but keep indefinitely.

'Flint Jack' the flint-knapper, Wiltshire, c. 1860

BEEF ROYAL

The Isles of Scilly (five in all) were once known as the Fortunate Isles and were settled in about 1700 B.C. by people from Brittany. The subtropical climate makes it into a spring bulb growers' paradise: most of the early daffodils, narcissus and jonquils sold in London and other cities are garnered from these peaceful and beautiful islands.

This Elizabethan recipe is delicious eaten cold and should be made the day before, so as to bring out the excellent flavour. It is very good for a buffet luncheon or supper.

5 lb. fillet or boned sirloin of beef	grated rind of $\frac{1}{2}$ lemon
2 pig's feet or $\frac{1}{2}$ calf's foot	1 glass port wine
(gelatine *can* be used, but the	salt and pepper
flavour will be impaired)	1 teaspoon chopped marjoram
$\frac{1}{2}$ bottle white wine	1 heaped tablespoon butter
5 slices lean ham	1 bayleaf
a pinch each of ground cloves,	3 pounded anchovy fillets
mace, nutmeg	3 chopped pickled walnuts

If using boned sirloin, cook the bones with the pigs' feet or calf's foot in the white wine, adding a very little water, to cover. Season to taste, and simmer for about 1 hour. Leave to get cold and strain, removing the fat. Cut the meat into 5 very thick slices and pound them. On top of each slice put a sprinkling of cloves, mace, nutmeg, lemon rind, marjoram and seasonings, then lay a slice of ham on top. Do this until the beef is back to its original shape, then skewer it well or tie it thoroughly so that it does not fall apart in cooking. Melt the butter and brown the meat on all sides. Put into a large saucepan or casserole, add the bayleaf and the strained stock. Cover, and cook very gently for 3-4 hours. Let it cool before taking out the beef. Put the meat into the deep dish it will be served from. When the stock has cooled, remove any fat, add the port and the pounded anchovies, boil it up, and let it bubble for 5-10 minutes. When slightly cooled, add the pickled walnuts, and pour the sauce gently over and around the beef. If serving cold, put into the refrigerator until the jelly has set. It is extremely good hot, but all the flavours are more discernible when it is cold. If using gelatine or aspic powder allow a level tablespoon to every $\frac{1}{2}$ pint of stock, or follow the instructions on the packet.

Serves about 10.

King Edward VII and escort, on the Isles of Scilly, 1902

FISH AND CHIPS

The catch always attracted great excitement, the leaping, silvery fish being quickly loaded into baskets, some to be salted, others to be hawked around the streets by fishwives, picturesque in their wide-brimmed black beaver hats and scarlet cloaks.

It is interesting to discover that the most English of foods does not appear in any early references until the latter half of the nineteenth century. Fried fish, to take away, is thought to have been brought to England by the large number of Italian immigrants who came at the time of the Risorgimento (1860), some of whom made a living with barrel organs and performing monkeys, some introduced the painted ice-cream cart (the hokey-pokey man), while others sold an anglicized form of *Fritto Misto de Mare*. Chips first appeared in Dundee about 1870, sold by a Belgian, Edward de Gurnier and his wife, who had a stall selling them with hot boiled peas, as they had been used to doing in Belgium. Who could ever have thought that such a felicitous marriage was in the offing? Freshly cooked fish and chips can be the most delicious of simple meals, like well-cooked eggs and bacon. The secret of doing it is as follows.

THE BATTER (for 4 medium fillets of fish)
4 oz. (1 cup) flour   ¼ cup cold water
½ teaspoon baking powder   salt and pepper

Mix the dry ingredients together and then beat in the water until it is the consistency of pancake batter. The baking powder is a trade secret, but if you want a puffy batter omit the baking powder, and at the last minute before using add the stiffly beaten white of egg. Dip the fish in the batter and fry in oil at 360°F. Do not use a basket for the fish only sticks to the mesh. Fish can be lightly fried until pale gold all over, then drained and re-fried when it is needed.

CHIPS, also known as 'French-fried' potatoes, should be of regular size and well soaked in water, to remove the starch, but they must be well-dried before cooking. Have the deep oil hot, but not smoking (try with a small piece of bread: if it sizzles, it is right), add the potatoes in a basket, and fry them lightly. Then drain them on paper, and when wanted, get the oil very hot, and re-fry them in small batches until they are the colour you like them. This second cooking makes them crisp and delicious. Serve hot from the pan.

Landing fish on Slapton Sands, Devon, c. *1900*

CHEESE STRAWS

The wondrous caves at Cheddar Gorge with their stalactites and stalagmites were all opened in the last century, mainly due to the vision of George Cox in 1837 and Richard Cox Gough and his sons in the 1890s. In 1903 a skeleton about 10,000 years old was unearthed as well as many Upper Palaeolithic flints, Baltic amber, axes and animal bones, pottery and a bone whistle from the much later Roman period. The two most famous caves bear the name of Gough and Cox and they are startling in their original beauty.

Cheddar is also world famous for its cheese, probably the most imitated cheese there is in the English-speaking world. None of the copies taste quite like the original, which is due to the particular water in the locality and the fertile soil. Its history goes back for centuries: Henry II bought eighty hundredweight of it and called it the 'best in England'. Henry III in 1253 granted a Charter for a weekly market and annual Fair which continued until the outbreak of World War I. In the seventeenth century all the neighbouring and adjoining parishes of Cheddar pooled their milk and made gigantic cheeses, sometimes reaching 100 pounds in weight, which would be matured for two to five years. Some 3,500 pounds were supplied by the parish for the Antarctic Expedition in 1901, and the largest Cheddar this century weighed 10 cwt., and was sent to the Wembley exhibition of 1924. Castle Cary is thought to make the finest Cheddar cheese today.

In East Brent, Somerset, there is a harvest home festival known as 'Bringing in the bread and cheese': a loaf 6 foot long and a 50–80 lb. cheese are carried shoulder-high by farmworkers early in September.

Cheese Straws are a feature of Cheddar and round about, and are still sold locally.

3 oz. (3 heaped tablespoons) butter or margarine	$\frac{1}{2}$ teaspoon mustard powder
4 oz. (1 cup) finely grated Cheddar cheese	1 egg, separated
	pinch of salt
3 oz. ($\frac{3}{4}$ cup) plain flour	pinch of cayenne pepper

Cream the butter and cheese, then add the sifted flour, cayenne, mustard powder and salt, and mix well. Add the beaten egg-yolk and mix into a stiff dough, then wrap in oiled paper and chill for 1 hour. Roll out on a lightly floured board to $\frac{1}{4}$-inch thickness, cut into 4-inch lengths, then into $\frac{1}{4}$-inch strips. Put onto a greased baking tray, brush with the lightly beaten egg-white and bake in a moderate oven (350°F.) for about 8–10 minutes. These tasty little straws can be served, warm, like little sticks, in thin napkin rings with clear soup, as well as for cocktail snacks.

Makes about 4 dozen.

SOMERSET RAREBIT

Put alternate layers of grated cheese and finely sliced onions in a greased pie dish. Do this twice, ending with a layer of cheese. Top with buttered breadcrumbs or crushed cream crackers and bake in a moderate oven (350°F.) for about 45 minutes. Serve with toast.

A covered carriage in Cheddar Gorge, c. *1890*

FILLET STEAKS WITH SHERRY AND CREAM SAUCE

'There were three sailors of Bristol City
Who took a boat and went to sea.
But first with beef and captain's biscuits
And pickled pork they loaded she.'

Little Billee, *William Makepeace Thackeray, 1811-1863*

4 thick fillet (tenderloin) steaks
4 large mushrooms
4 tablespoons cream
a dash of Worcestershire sauce
salt
freshly ground black pepper and
  peppercorns

$\frac{1}{4}$ pint ($\frac{1}{2}$ cup) dry sherry
2 oz. ($\frac{1}{4}$ cup) butter
1 tablespoon finely chopped
  chives
1 tablespoon finely chopped
  parsley

First marinate the steaks in the sherry with about 6 black peppercorns for at least 3 hours, turning them at least once. Then lift them out and pat them dry. Heat up the butter and lightly fry the large mushrooms so that they are soft but in no way crisp, then put them on to the serving dish and keep them warm. Fry the steaks to your liking: if very thick they will need about 3-4 minutes for rare steak, if about 2 inches thick, and correspondingly longer if liked well-done. When ready put them on top of the large mushrooms and keep warm. Then add the sherry marinade, Worcestershire sauce and herbs to the pan juices and reduce over a hot flame until about half the quantity. Season to taste, then add the cream, letting it come to just below boiling point, but stirring well so that the sauce is amalgamated. Serve over the steaks.

Serves 4.

This method is also very good for sweetbreads or brains, but first they must be boiled for about 20 minutes in water with a squeeze of lemon juice, drained, and when cold, the outer skin removed. Then proceed as above. About one pound of sweetbreads will serve 2 people, and at least 4 sets of brains are required.

T. Daniel & Sons' West India trader 'Maria' unloading at a berth on The Grove, Bristol, c. 1870

CHUDLEIGHS

Punch and Judy with the little dog Toby have amused children of all ages for centuries. The origin is obscure, but the story is attributed to Silvio Fiorillo, an Italian comedian of the seventeenth century: an allegory showing how Punch (or man) triumphs over all the ills and misfortunes. Samuel Pepys mentions in 1669 that some poor people had called their child Punch because it was fat; in 1703 Punch was introduced into a puppet play at Bartholomew Fair and from then on it has appeared in various puppet or marionette shows.

Chudleighs are a yeasted bun, sometimes called 'cut rounds' in North Devon, and 'splits' in the south. They are the same as Cornish Splits and are usually served hot, split open and sandwiched with raspberry or strawberry jam and clotted cream.

¼ oz. dried yeast	1 oz. (1 heaped tablespoon) lard
½ level teaspoon fine sugar	2 oz. (¼ cup) butter
¼ pint tepid water	1 lb. (4 cups) plain flour
6 tablespoons milk	a pinch of salt
jam and cream to serve with them	

Sprinkle the yeast and sugar over the tepid water and leave for 15 minutes or until it is covered with bubbles. Put the lard, butter and milk into a small saucepan and heat gently until the fat has melted, but on no account let it boil. Remove from the heat and let it cool. Sift the flour and salt into a mixing bowl, make a well in the centre and pour in the yeast mixture, then mix with the hands, until it is soft, but not sticky. Turn on to a floured board and knead for 5 minutes. Then put into a plastic bag, and leave in a warm place for 1 hour (or cover with a cloth). Remove from the bag and knead again for 5 minutes and divide into about 18 pieces. Knead each piece into a smooth ball, then place them on a lightly greased baking sheet ½ inch apart. Leave in a warm place until the buns are touching each other, then put into a preheated oven, 400°F., slightly above centre, and cook for 20 minutes or until well risen. They will sound hollow when tapped with the knuckles. Wrap in a cloth to keep them soft, if not serving at once. They can be warmed up in a slow oven before serving, split in half, and spread with jam and cream. If spread with clotted cream and treacle (molasses) they are known as 'Thunder and Lightning'.

Makes 18.

Watching the Punch and Judy Show, Ilfracombe, Devon, c. 1912

DORSET FLAN

Early in the 1890s Mary Salter, searching along the beach at Saltern Cove for corals, found alveolites (fossils). Thereupon many small 'fossil shops' sprang up all along the coast, and many survive to this day. The cliffs at Lyme Regis are of great geological interest.

Lyme Regis is also famous for a fourteenth-century quay called the Cobb which is 600 feet long; the Duke of Monmouth landed there in 1685 for his abortive rebellion against James II. It was also the scene of Louisa Musgrove's famous fall in Jane Austen's Persuasion.

FOR THE PASTRY	FOR THE FILLING
8 oz. (2 cups) flour	4 oz. cooked, sliced ham
4 oz. (1 cup) butter or margarine	3 eggs
4 tablespoons iced water (approx.)	½ pint (1 cup) milk
a pinch of salt	2 teaspoons fine semolina
	salt and pepper

First make the pastry by rubbing in the fat to the flour and salt, then add the water to make a smooth paste. Add a very little more if it is too dry. Grease an 8-inch flan tin (preferably with a removable base) and spread the rolled pastry over. Break one of the eggs, beat it well and brush the bottom of the pastry with a little beaten egg. (This prevents the bottom getting soggy.) Lay the ham slices over, and then break two whole unbeaten eggs on the top. Mix together in a basin the semolina, the milk and the remainder of the beaten egg, season to taste and mix it to a smooth paste. Pour this over the ham and egg, and bake in a moderately hot (375°F.) oven for 30-40 minutes, or until the top is nicely browned. Can be eaten either warm or cold.

Serves 4.

Traditionally this would be served with 'Darzet' watercress and followed by very crisp little rusk-like rolls called Dorset knobs with Blue Vinny cheese. Blue Vinny (vinny from *vinid* meaning 'mouldy') is a quite exceptional blue cheese always made in farm-houses. Now, unfortunately, it is not generally on sale, but there are certain pubs which serve it: you have to keep your ear very close to the ground to hunt them out, but it is well worth the effort.

Fossil Shop, Lyme Regis, Dorset, c. 1892

MARKET DAY CASSEROLE

Hiring Fairs were an annual fixture in every important country town until early in this century. The men and maids seeking work stood in rows and the masters and mistresses walked down the lines selecting those who suited them. A few days after the hiring or Statute Fair it was customary to hold a Mop Fair, so called because those seeking work wore tufts or tassels denoting their calling: thus a cowherd wore a tuft of hair from a cow's tail; a carter wore whipcord on his hat, and a maid servant would carry a feather duster and so on. Another explanation for the name is the old country name of 'mop' being a word for a fool, the Mop Fair being the last chance for those who were too dull or slovenly to be hired at the Statute Fair.

Gloucestershire is famous for its apples and the Gloucester Old Spot pig, a black and white dappled breed, for centuries fattened on fallen apples which gives it a delectable flavour. Gloucester was also the meeting place for the huge West Country drove routes. Mixed herds of cattle met from Wales and beyond Hereford. The dark blackish-brown Old Gloucester cow, primarily a dairy breed, indicates influence from the black Welsh cattle.

6 trimmed pork chops (without bone)
2 pigs' kidneys
1 lb. onions, peeled and sliced
1 teaspoon chopped sage
salt and pepper

3 medium apples, peeled, cored and sliced
1½ lb. peeled, sliced potatoes
1 cup cider, or stock
1 cup water

Put a layer of sliced potatoes and onions on the bottom of a deep casserole and season to taste. Then a layer of the chops and the kidneys, which have been skinned and sliced. On top put the sliced apples and the sage. Then repeat the onion, meats and potato but keep back enough potato for a thick layer on top. Season each layer well, pour over the cider or stock and water and put the lid on, first rubbing it over with some butter or margarine so that it doesn't stick. Cook in a slow oven (250°F.) for 2½ hours; in fact the longer it is cooked, within reason, the more savoury it will be. Remove the lid for the last half-hour to let the top brown slightly.

Serves 6-8.

KIDDLEY BROTH

The Man-engine was a perilous means of lowering men into very deep mines, and was discontinued by about 1912, for it needed expert co-operation to avoid accidents. Dolcoath, the deepest, widest and richest tin and copper mine in Cornwall, produced over 5½ million pounds of ore in 1882, but this wealth was not passed on to the miners who lived in conditions of extreme poverty at near starvation level. Famine fare of Cornish miners about 1860 has been described thus: '. . . For dinner we had a barley pastie with two bits of pork on potatoes, and for supper a barley cake, or potatoes or turnips with a barley cover.' Many thousands of miners emigrated to open up mines in Peru, California, and Australia: Cornish miners were to be found literally all over the world, from Chile to Nova Scotia and from Cuba to the Rand and India. They became known as 'Cousin Jacks', for whenever a job fell vacant, the fortunate ones were quick to suggest a 'cousin' back home. To this day the Colorado Folk-lore Society in the United States holds a Cornish dinner on the Eve of St Piran's Day, serving traditional Cornish food. St Piran, the patron saint of 'tinners', floated across from Ireland and died in A.D. 550, having first dug his own grave.

By 1900, there were only a handful of tin mines surviving in Cornwall, but this was compensated for, to some extent, by the rise in production of Cornish china clay (formed by the decomposition of granite) previously found only in its pure state in few places, mainly China.

Kiddley Broth (also called Kettle Broth) gives an idea of the sparse diet for hard-working men. It consists of bread cut into squares, a few marigold flower heads and a handful of chopped three-cornered leek leaves (this is a plant common in Cornwall, looking like a white bluebell, with three-cornered leaves; the taste is like wild garlic), a lump of butter, or dripping or bacon rinds, pepper and salt, all put into a basin with boiling water poured over it. Nowadays it is made with leeks or onions and good stock.

LIKKY PIE

(Leek Pie) was served on high days and holidays and is extremely good.

12 cleaned and chopped leeks
½ lb. sliced unsmoked bacon
¼ pint (½ cup) cream
8 oz. shortcrust pastry (see page 54)

2 eggs, separated
¼ pint (½ cup) milk
salt and pepper

Put the cleaned chopped leeks in the milk with seasonings and cook for 5 minutes only, then lift them out with a slice and layer them with the bacon in a pie-dish until the dish is filled. Add the milk and cover with the pastry crust and bake for ½ hour at 350°F. Then remove from the oven, lift off the crust carefully and take out some of the liquid. Beat the egg-yolks and cream together, then add the stiffly beaten whites and put this on top; then put the crust back and bake again in the oven (with a foil cover over the pastry if it is getting too brown) for 10 minutes. Personally I prefer it without the pastry crust, when it comes out like a delicious kind of leek soufflé.

Serves 4-6.

The Man-engine in operation at Dolcoath Mine,
Camborne, Cornwall, c. 1893

DORSET JUGGED STEAK

'The Fair Day is to the milk-maids and striplings of some villages one of the brightest in their calendar ... Some time ago, on a fine day in September, I went to a famous fair, held at the foot of one of the green hills of Dorset ... I was this time in the fair, where the din of drums and horns at the shows, the loud invitation, "Walk up, walk up", of the showmen, the hum of voices, the squeaking of fiddles, and the creaking of rattles, made altogether a medley of sounds ...' Some Dorset Folklore, from Hone's Year Book, *1822. The Reverend William Barnes (the Dorset Poet), 1800-86.*

> *'If you in Do'set be a-roamen,*
> *An' ha' business at a farm*
> *Then woon't ye see your eale a-foamen,*
> *Or your cider down to warm?*
> *Woon't ye have brown bread a-put ye?*
> *An' some venny cheese ent ye?*
> *Butter? Rolls o't!*
> *Cream? Why bowls o't!'*

William Barnes

A Dorset Feast, spelt 'Veast', would undoubtedly have contained 'Lamb's Tail Pie' made from the curious Dorset Horn sheep which have horn-rimmed 'spectacles' on! Lambs' tail pie consisted of layers of lambs' tails, with bacon, sliced hard-boiled eggs, fresh herbs, lemon peel and seasoning, all covered with stock and pastry. It was eaten hot, or cold and jellied. Cabbage was first planted in Dorset: ''Tis scarce 100 years since we had Cabbages out of Holland,

Sir Arthur Ashley, of Wilburg St. Giles, in Dorsetshire, being the first who planted them in England.' A gardener's book of 1699.

3 lb. chopped stewing steak (preferably shin, for flavour)	1 large sliced onion
	6 cloves
½ lb. sausagemeat	¼ pint (1 cup) port wine
1 cup breadcrumbs	1 tablespoon redcurrant jelly
1 egg	1 tablespoon chopped parsley
1 tablespoon flour	salt and pepper

Cut the steak into cubes and roll in the flour, then put into a casserole. Add the onion, cloves, parsley, port and water to cover, seasoning to taste. Cover, and cook gently in a slow to moderate oven (300°F.) for about 2½ hours, checking that the liquid has not run dry and topping up with a little water if it has. Meanwhile mix together the sausagemeat, breadcrumbs and the beaten egg, seasoning to taste. Flour your hands and roll this mixture into very small balls, then poach these balls in boiling water for about 10 minutes, skimming them off after this time. First stir in the redcurrant jelly to the steak, and then add the balls. Leave the lid off and continue cooking for a further 15 minutes. Stock or a mixture of water and stock can be used instead of port if preferred.

Serves 6-8.

Woodbury Hill Fair, Dorset, c. 1900, photographer Charles Hankinson (the author Clive Holland)

MENDIP SNAILS

Herbert Ernest Balch (probably from the Welsh bwlch, a mountain pass) was the pioneer of Mendip Cave exploration as we know it. Writing in 1906 he says: 'From the time when, twenty years ago, in the ancient Hyaena Den of Wookey Hole, I stopped and picked up the broken fragment of a Reindeer antler, I have been a consistent explorer of these wonderful caverns . . .' He founded the Wells Museum in 1893 and was Honorary Curator for sixty years. It was at Lamb Leer that he nearly lost his life, being lowered down on a rotten rope which broke and caused him to fall 65 feet into the Great Chamber. Many years later he was to say to a friend 'that he had nightmares repeating the fall and pain in the hand, decreasing in frequency until they ceased after perhaps two years'. Yet he was to write: 'Lamb Leer . . . that most wonderful of all wonderful caverns.'

In Roman times Priddy was the centre of the lead-mining industry. Priddy Sheep Fair (3rd Wednesday in August), which has been going for over 600 years and was moved from Wells at the time of the Black Death, still goes on. Mendip snails, known locally as 'wallfish' are a speciality of the district, and thought to be a heritage from Roman times. Mr Paul Leyton, who owns the 'Miner's Arms', a most excellent restaurant near Priddy, cooks them in the following way.

Mendip snails, ordinary garden snails, *Helix aspersa*, are excellent for use. Allow at least 12-18 per person. Immerse the snails in water to which a tablespoon of salt per gallon has been added. After 6 hours add 2 more tablespoons salt, and after another 6 hours or overnight 2 tablespoons more. Cover, and leave for 36 hours, when they will be dead.

Put on the stove 2 large saucepans half full with 6 cups (3 pints) boiling water, then put the snails in for 5 minutes, first in one saucepan with 1 tablespoon salt, then in the other, during which time the water must be boiling furiously. This cleans the snails and 2 saucepans are necessary, one as a wash, and the other as a rinse. Drain, and rinse under a cold tap. They are now ready to be simmered and served with their sauce.

COURT BOUILLON (for 6 dozen snails)

4 cups water	3 small sliced onions
2 cups dry cider or white wine	3 small sliced carrots
2 bayleaves	4 cloves
a sprig of tarragon	pepper and salt

Bring all ingredients to the boil, add the snails and simmer slowly for 4 hours. Then remove to cool, mouth down on a wire rack.

FOR THE SAUCE

½ lb. (1 cup) butter	1 teaspoon each dill, fennel,
2 tablespoons Cheddar cheese,	chervil, chives, balm
grated	½ teaspoon each lemon thyme
2 tablespoons cream	and ground black pepper
½ teaspoon each salt and cayenne	

Beat all ingredients together and gently warm. To fill the snails with the sauce, hold in the left hand and nearly pull it out of the shell, then force the sauce in with a teaspoon. Press back and place mouth up until the sauce sets. To serve, put onto a snail plate and heat, either under a hot grill or in a hot oven (425°F.) for 10 minutes. Serve with brown bread.

Early 'Cavers', Lamb Leer, near Priddy, Somerset, c. 1900. Photograph by H. E. Balch (1869-1958)

GLOUCESTER CHEESE AND ALE

Traditional

Gloucester cheese was first made in the eighteenth century in the Vale of Gloucester and the Vale of Berkeley from the milk of Old Gloucester cows. It is made in two colours, pale yellow and red, and in two varieties, single and double. Double Gloucester is quite delicious, with a mild, creamy flavour, and a soft yet firm texture. It is equally good for eating plain, or when a little stale, for cooking. Single Gloucester has an open texture and is soft: excellent in its way, and not to be compared with the Double Gloucester cheese, which is more matured.

½ lb. Gloucester cheese (Cheddar or Cheshire can also be used)
½ pint strong ale or dark beer
6 slices brown toasted bread

1 tablespoon strong made English mustard (or according to taste)

Cut the cheese into thin flakes and put into a fireproof dish spread with the mustard. Pour over the ale, to cover, then bake in a hot oven for about ½ hour or until it is soft and melted. Have ready the brown toast and moisten it with a little more ale, then pour over the hot cheese and serve with pickles and more beer.

THE QUEEN'S TOASTED CHEESE
(from the Royal Lodge, Windsor, 1869)

'Grate half a pound of cheese very fine and add to it three table-spoonfuls of ale and a small glass of champagne. Mix it well in a silver dish over a lamp for ten minutes and serve it in the dish as hot as possible, with a plate of thin hot toast.'

A West Country man with friends, c. 1890

MATRIMONY CAKE

Wishing wells are quite common in this part of the country; in Ireland they would be called Holy wells, but no doubt the pilgrims wished for very much the same things. Matrimonial oracles are traditional to Dorset and take many forms throughout the year. On Midsummer Eve a girl would put her shoes in the form of a T and say this rhyme:

> 'Hoping this night my true love to see,
> I place my shoes in the form of a T.'

An apple pip is often used by girls as a test of their lover's faithfulness. If on putting it on the fire it bursts with the heat she is assured of his affection: but if it burns silently it means he is false. Whilst anxiously waiting, the following rhyme is chanted:

> 'If you love me, pop and fly;
> If you hate me lay and die.'

Yet another oracle takes place with an even ash-leaf which is placed in the hand and the following said:

> 'The even ash-leaf in my hand,
> The first I meet shall be my man.'

It is then transferred to the glove, with:

> 'The even ash-leaf in my glove,
> The first I meet shall be my love.'

Finally it is placed in the bosom, with the words:

> 'The even ash-leaf in my bosom,
> The first I meet shall be my husband.'

Matrimony Cake: recipe from 1800

8 oz. shortcrust pastry (see page 54)
4 tablespoons brown breadcrumbs
4 large peeled and cored apples
4 tablespoons of mixed currants, chopped candied peel and seedless raisins
½ teaspoon nutmeg and ground ginger, mixed
juice of 1 lemon, and 1 large slice of lemon
2 tablespoons sugar
2 tablespoons golden syrup (corn syrup)

Cut the pastry into two and roll them out to fit a greased 8-inch flan tin. Lay one round over the flan tin and on top put the rings of cored apples, overlapping on top. Add all the other ingredients evenly, and place the slice of lemon in the middle. Damp the edges, and cover with the remaining pastry, pressing down the edges very well. Brush over with a little milk and bake for ½ hour in a moderate (350°F.) oven, or until the top is golden brown. It is usually eaten hot with Devonshire cream.

Serves 4.

The Wishing Well, Upwey, Dorset, c. 1890

WEST COUNTRY BAKED PILCHARDS

This rhyme came about because large quantities of pilchards were exported to Italy and many other Mediterranean countries. The pilchard (Sardina pilchardus) at a later stage of growth is simply another name for a sardine, hence the shipping of these fish to Italy, France and Portugal. Because of their high fat content they travel badly, which is why both the young (sardine) and old (pilchard) are canned. The shoals appear without warning, and only briefly: they also disappear for some years, as happened in the 1920s in Cornwall. Anyone who has tasted the delights of freshly grilled sardines will know what a fresh pilchard is like. A Cornish name for them is 'Fair Maids', possibly a corruption of the Spanish fumade *(smoked) from the time when Spanish fishing fleets assembled off the Cornish coast. It is possible that many of the curious sunken pits to be seen in Cornwall were used for smoking these in early times.*

Despite the vast numbers caught, economic conditions in Cornwall in the last century made them a luxury for the poor. When available, they were served simmered with potatoes in thin cream (the rich clotted cream being an expensive luxury) and it was called 'Dippy'.

Stargazey pie was another method of serving: the fish were stuffed with chopped herbs and spice, then arranged on pastry with the heads to the outside; bits of chopped bacon and onion were scattered around and the whole covered with a mixture of eggs and cream, then covered with pastry, so that the heads protruded on the outside, hence the name.

WEST COUNTRY BAKED PILCHARDS
(also for herrings and mackerel)

8 pilchards, cleaned and filleted	½ pint (1 cup) pale beer
1 teaspoon each of ground cloves and allspice	½ pint (1 cup) vinegar
1 medium sliced onion	4 bayleaves
	black pepper and salt

Salt and spice each fish, roll them and lay in an ovenproof dish. Scatter the onion and bayleaves around and plenty of black pepper. Pour over the mixed beer and vinegar (if using stronger beer, make it two-thirds beer and one-third vinegar), cover and bake in a moderate oven (350°F.) for about 1 hour. They are excellent either cold or hot.

Serves 4.

Salted fish in barrels, The Basin, Penzance, Cornwall, 1900

HAM OLIVE PIE

Stonehenge, which comes from the Saxon word Stanhengist, *meaning 'hanging stones' is at the same time one of the wonders and mysteries of Great Britain. This prehistoric monument has been in turn described as a Bronze Age temple, or palace; a temple or observatory for the Druids; even as a headquarters for the many herding and farming communities that existed on and around the plain. It was probably begun about 1850 B.C. and added to in the Bronze Age (1500 to 1000 B.C.). Sir Edmund Antrobus gained legal title to it in 1905, but the family subsequently sold it to the Government. It dominates the surrounding plain with its magnificent and mysterious qualities. Nearby in Avebury is a similar monument although the stones are smaller.*

Wiltshire ham and bacon is mild-cured and delicious; the following is an old Wiltshire method of pickling and curing.

Boil together: 1½ lb. of cooking salt, 4 oz. saltpetre, 2 oz. salt prunella, ½ oz. juniper berries, 2 lb. treacle (molasses), ½ lb. bay salt, 1 oz. black peppercorns and 2 quarts of beer. First sprinkle the pork ham with salt and leave for 12 hours then wipe it dry. Pour over the above pickle when slightly cooled and leave for a month, turning the ham daily and rubbing the pickle well into the skin. Dry well before storing. When cooking, soak overnight in cold water, and leave in the cooking liquid when done, for 2 hours.

HAM OLIVE PIE

Adapted from a recipe in *The Compleat Servant-Maid*, 1677.

1 lb. ham cut into medium slices	2 teaspoons each of chopped lovage and parsley
3 hard-boiled eggs, separated	6 gooseberries
12 stoned dates	1 tablespoon caster (extrafine) sugar
a pinch of nutmeg and pinch of cinnamon	2 tablespoons butter
2 tablespoons currants	salt and pepper
12 button mushrooms	a little milk
½ pint (1 cup) cider	
8 oz. shortcrust pastry (see page 54)	

Mix together the hard-boiled egg-yolks and all the other ingredients, chopped very finely, *except* the ham, cider, egg-whites, milk and butter. Cut the ham into 4-inch squares and fill each slice with the above mixture. Roll up these 'olives' and place them close together in a deep pie-dish. Pour over the cider, add the chopped egg-whites and dot with butter. Moisten the edges of the pie-dish and cover with the pastry. Brush the top with a little milk and bake in a moderate oven (350°F.) for about 45 minutes. The pie can be eaten hot or cold.

Serves 4-6.

This pie can also be made with thin slices of raw veal, which should be beaten flat before filling with the fruit and egg stuffing.

Conversation piece at Stonehenge, Salisbury Plain, Wiltshire, c. *1872*

RED MULLET

In the last century Weymouth was renowned for its mullet, both red and grey. The Duke of Portland used to go there especially for this delicacy. The medium-sized fish were available for threepence or four-pence each, but His Grace had been known to pay two guineas for one weighing a pound and a half. His custom was to put all the livers together in a butter boat. Weymouth is still renowned for the quality of its fish, and a speciality is made of red mullet, John Dory and especially of lobster.

RED MULLET cooked in paper
Also for John Dory fillets, plaice, haddock or hake fillets. Foil can be used instead of oiled paper.

Red Mullet is known as the 'woodcock of the sea', which means that the entrails are eaten as in woodcock. When cleaning, remove only the gills.

2 small or 1 large fish per person is an average helping.

4 large red mullet rolled in flour	1 chopped mushroom per fish
1 small sliced shallot or 1 slice onion per fish	1 tablespoon sherry per fish
	1 small nut of butter per fish
1 teaspoon each of chopped parsley and fennel per fish	salt and a pinch of cayenne pepper

Take 4 pieces of oiled paper or foil large enough to cover the fish completely and wrap them well up. Butter the foil with half the butter and place the fish on top. Add all the other ingredients to each package, then fold and secure it well on top. Put into a baking tin and bake in a moderate oven (350°F.) for ½ hour. Serve each fish in its paper, and also a small jug of melted butter flavoured with a touch of anchovy essence and a good squeeze of lemon. The fish can also be baked without being individually wrapped, using the same ingredients, but a piece of foil should be put over the top while cooking.

Donkey rides at Weymouth, Dorset, c. 1889

SOMERSET BRAISED LAMB

Yeovil has a flourishing glove-making industry which is over 350 years old. It is also noted for black and white sheep, known as 'Jacob's sheep'; legend has it that they came from a wrecked Armada ship.

This is also an excellent recipe for a joint of boiling bacon or ham. If using ham or bacon trim the joint of fat before cooking.

4 lb. joint lean lamb, either leg
   or best end of neck
3 bayleaves
6 black peppercorns
1 tablespoon fat or oil
1 large sliced onion
3 carrots and 3 turnips, sliced
2 leeks

1 tablespoon currants and 1
   tablespoon seedless raisins or
   sultanas
3 cloves
1 cup lamb stock
½ pint (1 cup) cider
salt

Put the lamb into cold water to half-way up, add the bayleaves and peppercorns, cover and simmer gently for ½ hour. Meanwhile, heat the oil or fat in an ovenproof dish and gently sauté the vegetables until they are soft but not coloured. Put the lamb on top, with a skimmed cupful of the stock and the cider. Then add the fruit, cloves and a little salt. Cover and bake in a moderate oven (350°F.) for 2½ hours. Before serving put the joint onto a warmed serving dish with the vegetables and sauce around the joint.

Serves about 8.

Lizzie Little wins the Donkey Derby, near Yeovil, 1897

DORSET SAUSAGE

Bere Regis is in the heart of Thomas Hardy's country as portrayed in his books. This ancient town held a royal residence in Saxon times, hence its name. The splendid church with its carved and painted roof contains the tombs of the Turbervilles, the name used by Hardy for his immortal novel, Tess of the d'Urbervilles.

'*. . . so before starting we'll one and all come to my house and have a rasher of bacon; then every man-jack get a pint of cider into his inside; then we'll warm up an extra drop wi' some mead and a bit of ginger; everyone take a thimbleful . . . to finish off his inner man – Why sonnies a man's not himself till he is fortified wi' a bit and a drop?'* Under the Greenwood Tree, *Thomas Hardy, 1872.*

DORSET SAUSAGE

Recipe of Mrs Thomas Hardy, Max Gate, Dorchester. This is very like a coarse terrine, or a meat loaf, and is eaten cold, in slices.

1 lb. minced beef	1 small nutmeg, grated
1 lb. minced ham or shoulder or cushion of bacon	½ teaspoon ground mace
	2 eggs, well beaten
6 oz. (2 cups) fresh breadcrumbs	salt and pepper

Mix the meats together thoroughly, then add the breadcrumbs and mix again. Stir in the eggs and seasonings, and either put into a large damp cloth and tie securely, then boil in water to cover for 3 hours, or bake in a greased cake tin for about 1½ hours. Leave to get quite cold before turning out. Then either scatter with toasted crumbs, or pour over a little made aspic to glaze it. It is very good for a picnic, or a cold supper.

Serves about 6-8.

DORSET APPLE CAKE

½ lb. peeled, cored and chopped apples	½ lb. (2 cups) flour
4 oz. (½ cup) lard or margarine	4 oz. (½ cup) sugar
1½ teaspoons baking powder	1 egg *or* 3 tablespoons milk
	a pinch of salt

Rub the fat into the salt and the flour, then add the baking powder. Mix the sugar with the apples and stir into the flour mixture, then make a firm dough with either the beaten egg or the milk. Grease a round flat tin and put the mixture in, about 1 inch thick, then bake in a moderate oven (350°F.) for 45–60 minutes. Cut open and spread with butter whilst hot. 2 tablespoons of currants or raisins can be added if liked.

Setting off for the day from Bere Regis, Dorset, c. 1895
Photograph by Charles Hankinson
(Clive Holland, who wrote a biography of his friend Thomas Hardy)

POTATOES AND SPICES

Devonport is part of the Borough of Plymouth, where Sir Francis Drake played out his game of bowls at the Hoe while the Spanish Armada sailed to meet him; it was from Plymouth that the Mayflower *set out for the New World with the brave Devonians and East Anglians who were to colonize New England.*

Drake, Raleigh, Hawkins and Frobisher were all men of Devon and it is due to their adventurous bravery that the eating habits of the English were changed in the sixteenth century. Drake and Hawkins brought back the first sweet potatoes to England about 1563-5. They quickly superseded the parsnip which had been traditionally always eaten with roast beef. The first ordinary potatoes were brought back by Raleigh after his expedition to North Carolina in 1585, and they were thought to have been traded for by the settlers from the Spaniards. Drake said of the sweet potato:

'These potatoes be the most delicate rootes that may be eaten, and doe farre exceed our passeneps or carets. Their pines be of the bignes of two fists, the outside whereof is of the making of a pine-apple, but it is soft like the rinde of a Cucomber, and the inside eateth like an apple but it is more delicious than any sweet apple sugred.'

Much of the incentive for exploration (and the money which financed these expeditions) came from a desire to discover the source of spices and herbs which for centuries had come overland across the Middle East, or across the Indian Ocean to Arabia. As a result they were very expensive by the time they reached Europe. By finding the source it was possible to bring them directly back, thus cutting out the innumerable middlemen. Citrus fruits and many other foods vital to health were more readily available. Thus those brave sea-dogs might also be called food explorers, and it is worth remembering this as we put a pinch of cinnamon, mace or other spice into our dishes.

Cornwall Beach, Devonport, Plymouth, Devon, c. 1895

WHITE POT

Feasts or 'Revels' are a feature of the West Country. A relic of the Middle Ages, they are still held annually in many villages. Avening in Gloucestershire has an annual feast at which pig's head (see Brawn, page 1) is served; Cranham holds a feast each August with roast venison as the traditional dish; Painswick, a beautiful village in Gloucestershire, with ninety-nine yew trees in the churchyard, has an annual 'Clipping Feast' in September, when children circle the church and afterwards are given buns. It is a harvest festival of pagan origin. Legend has it that despite all attempts to grow one hundred yew trees, one will always wither and die. The devil will come in the night and take its life.

White Pot (sometimes spelt White Put) is a feature of many feasts or revels. The following amount makes a large quantity, and should be halved if not more than 6 persons are being served.

4 quarts milk	2 oz. (¼ cup) butter
1 lb. (4 cups) flour	1 nutmeg finely grated
1 lb. golden (or light corn) syrup	½ teaspoon mixed spice
8 eggs	¾ pint (1½ cups) cold water

Beat up the eggs with the flour, warmed syrup and spices. Boil the milk and stir, still boiling, into these ingredients, forming a well-mixed paste. Pour into an oven proof earthenware or glass container. Dot the butter on top, and just before putting in the oven pour the cold water into the middle and bake without stirring in a moderate oven (350°F.) for the first hour, and in a slow (225°F.) oven for a further 6 hours. It is eaten either cold or warm. If making the half quantity cook for only 3½ hours.

CHEESECAKE

was always a traditional feature of Frampton-on-Severn Feast.

CRUST

4 oz. crushed digestive or sweet biscuits

2 oz. (¼ cup) butter, melted (shortcrust pastry can be used if preferred)

FILLING

1 lb. (4 cups) cottage cheese

2 tablespoons sultanas or seedless raisins

3 separated eggs

½ pint (1 cup) sour cream

4 heaped tablespoons caster sugar

1 tablespoon cornflour

a few drops of vanilla essence, or use vanilla sugar instead of caster sugar

Well grease an 8-inch loose-bottomed tin, and coat base and sides with the biscuits mixed with the melted butter, pressing down very well. Beat the egg-yolks with the sugar, add the beaten cheese, cornflour, sour cream, flavouring, and sultanas. Beat the egg-whites until stiff and fold in. Pour into the biscuit case and bake until golden brown in a moderate oven (350°F.) for about 1 hour. Let it cool completely before turning out.

Serves 6.

The 'Ghost Exhibition' at Frampton Feast, Gloucestershire, 1887

SOMERSET APPLE CAKE

The Hobby Horse festival common to Minehead and Padstow (Cornwall) takes place on May Day and is a relic of the Celtic horse worship connected with the ancient King of May. May Day eve is known as 'warning night' and the horse, attendants and 'Gullivers' (masked men who follow the hobby horse) go to a crossroads at Whitecross, where the horse dances. These celebrations go on until 3rd May. Although basically connected with fertility for the coming year, the festival was also associated with frightening away the enemy (in this case the invading Danes about A.D. 800) from Minehead; thus it is brought out as a celebration by the sailors. As recently as 1956 bunches of primroses were put into cows' stalls, and branches of greenery were hung over the threshold last thing at night on May day eve.

'For O, For O, the hobby-horse is forgot.' Shakespeare.

SOMERSET APPLE CAKE

½ lb. (2 cups) flour
½ teaspoon mixed spice
3 heaped tablespoons butter or margarine
3 heaped tablespoons caster (extrafine) sugar

1 lb. peeled, cored and finely chopped apples
1 beaten egg
a little milk
coarse sugar for garnishing

Grease and line an 8-inch cake tin with greaseproof paper. Sift the flour into a bowl with the spices and blend in the butter until the mixture resembles breadcrumbs. Stir in the caster sugar and the chopped apples. Add the beaten egg to make a spreading mixture. If it seems too dry, add a little milk. Turn into the lined tin and bake at 375°F. for 1 to 1¼ hours, or until firm to the touch. Turn onto a wire tray, remove the paper, and serve either hot or cold. Dredge with the coarse sugar before serving, and, if serving hot, serve cream with the cake.

Apples are an important feature of Somerset life and the apple harvest goes on until November. They are used on Christmas Eve for a drink called Lamb's Wool, which is ale heated with a pinch of mixed spice, served with apples roasted with cloves stuck in them, and accompanied by nuts and hot cakes. In January the apple trees are regaled with song, whilst the singers drink cider in wassail cups, to assure a good crop for the year. When the apples are picked, the little ones are left on for the pixies.

HARD SAUCE

for serving with baked apples

4 oz. (½ cup) butter
1 stiffly beaten egg-white

4 oz. (½ cup) sugar
1 teaspoon grated nutmeg

Cream the butter and sugar very well, then fold in the stiffly beaten egg-white. Sprinkle the nutmeg over the top, chill, and serve with the hot apples. Makes 1½ cups sauce.

The Minehead sailors' Hobby Horse, Quay Street, Minehead, Somerset, 1900

HITE FOAM SOUP

1½ oz. (3 tablespoons) butter
1 oz. (1 heaped tablespoon) flour
1 quart (4 cups) milk, warmed
1 large clove, crushed garlic
1 medium, peeled and sliced
  onion
4 slices crustless bread fried in
  oil, then cut up for croûtons

1 cup chopped celery
1 small piece blade mace or a
  pinch of powdered mace
2 eggs, separated
2 oz. (1 cup) grated cheese
1 tablespoon chopped parsley
salt and pepper

Melt the butter and stir in the flour, and when slightly browned add the milk, gradually, stirring well all the time until the sauce is smooth. Let it simmer gently, then add the garlic, onion, celery and mace, cover and simmer for 30 minutes. Cool slightly, then add the well-beaten yolks, heat but do not reboil. Add the seasoning to taste and the grated cheese, stir well and keep warm. Beat the egg-whites, and fold half into the soup, put the rest into the tureen or soup bowl and pour the hot soup over. Sprinkle with parsley and serve with croûtons.

Serves 4-6.

GLOUCESTER FOWL PIE

1 3-lb. chicken cut into joints
2 medium chopped onions
½ lb. diced ham or bacon
1 small head celery, chopped
3 tablespoons chopped parsley
3 sliced hard-boiled eggs

a pinch of mace
1 teaspoon chopped thyme
10 white peppercorns (whole)
salt
8 oz. shortcrust pastry (see page
  54)

Barely cover all ingredients except the ham, eggs and parsley with cold water, bring to the boil and simmer very gently for about 1 hour or until tender. Leave to get cold, then take the skin from the bird and also the bones, remove all fat from the stock. Put the chicken in a deep pie-dish layered with the ham, 3 sliced hard-boiled eggs and 3 tablespoons chopped fresh parsley. Cover with the jellied stock and season to taste. Moisten the edges of the pie-dish and cover with pastry (see page 54), brush the top with milk and bake in a moderate oven (350°F.) for about ½ hour or until golden. It is equally good hot, or cold, when it will be a thick jelly.

Serves about 6.

New Inn courtyard, c. 1870.
New Inn still stands in Gloucester
and looks very much the same
from the outside.

BATH BUNS

'Oh! who can ever be tired of Bath?' Northanger Abbey, Jane Austen, 1818.

This beautiful city has been famous since it was the Roman city of Aquae Sulis for its medicinal waters, and since the eighteenth century for its elegance as well. The overeating and excess drinking of the period was remedied by drinking pure mineral waters, but as many people came to see the fashionable company, such characters as Beau Nash and Beau Brummell, as to get cured of their gout or other afflictions. Many writers such as Jane Austen, Smollett, Fielding and Dickens have given vivid pictures of Bath at various times. The Pump Room became a fashionable meeting-place, not only for rich Londoners, but for mothers with pretty daughters to marry off! The food has always been noted: the best meat from Wales; the finest fish from Dorset and Cornwall; cider from Somerset; apricots, cherries and plums from the warm garden walls of the Cotswolds, and the finest cream and butter from Devon. Bath Olivers (the finest biscuits for eating with cheese, made by Dr Oliver), Bath Chaps (the cheek and tongue of the local, long-jawed, fruit-fed pigs, smoked and cooked ready to serve); Bath York-House ham, cooked in the 'wort' of malt used for brewing; the fried gudgeon; Bath buns, which became popular in London as well, all are famous.

'After the play I came home, ate a Bath cake and a sweet orange, and went comfortably to bed.' Boswell's London Journal, 1762-3.

BATH BUNS

$\frac{3}{4}$ oz. yeast creamed with 1 teaspoon sugar
$\frac{1}{2}$ pint (1 cup) warm milk
1 lb. (4 cups) flour
a pinch of salt
8 tablespoons butter
4 oz. ($\frac{1}{2}$ cup) caster (extrafine) sugar
3 small beaten eggs
2 heaped tablespoons chopped candied peel
2 oz. ($\frac{1}{2}$ cup) crushed lump sugar (for finish)

Add the creamed yeast to the warm (tepid) milk, pour into the warmed flour and salt and knead lightly. Cream the butter with the caster sugar and add the eggs. Work these into the dough, with the peel, keeping back a little for top decoration. Cover, and put to rise in a warm place for 40 minutes. Shape into little buns, put them on a greased baking sheet and brush with a little sweetened milk or egg, sprinkle with the crushed sugar, finally decorating each with a piece of peel. Bake in a moderate oven (350°F.) for about $\frac{1}{2}$ hour.

Makes about 12.

Grand Pump Room and Library, Abbey Churchyard west side, with Bath chairs, Bath, Somerset, c. 1890

POOR MAN'S GOOSE

John Gay, who was born in Barnstable, Devon, in 1685, spent some time at Amesbury Abbey as a guest of the Earl of Queensbury. There is a small Queen Anne folly in the park where he is said to have written the successful Beggar's Opera, which made 'Rich gay, and Gay rich'.

A favourite countryman's recipe

1½ lb. lamb's liver
½ lb. bacon in the piece, but chopped in dice
1 lamb's heart
2 large onions
2 lb. potatoes

pinch powdered sage
½ teaspoon of chopped parsley and thyme mixed
1 cup meat stock
salt and pepper

Cut the liver and cleaned heart in thick slices; peel and slice the onions and potatoes. In a large ovenproof dish put a layer of potatoes, then meat, then the onion and diced bacon, seasoning each layer and adding a sprinkling of herbs. Repeat this until the ingredients are finished, ending with a layer of potatoes. Pour over the stock, cover and bake in a moderate oven (350°F.) for 2 hours. Serve with apple sauce.

Serves 4-6.

DEVIZES PIE was a traditional Wiltshire dish, now

seldom seen even in private houses. It consisted of slices of cold, cooked calf's head, sliced cold lamb, calf's brains, sliced tongue and rashers of bacon, all put into a pie-dish with several sliced hard-boiled eggs, a pinch of spice, cayenne pepper, and salt, covered with stock that would jelly, and a pastry crust on top. It was baked for about 1 hour, then turned out when cold.

STIR-IN-PUDDING is another country favourite.

12 oz. self-raising flour
4 oz. (½ cup) sugar
¼ pint (½ cup) milk

6 oz. lard or margarine
½ lb. gooseberries or rhubarb

Rub the fat into the flour, add sugar and stir in the fruit, then stir in the milk, to make a fairly stiff mixture. Put into a greased basin, tie down and steam for 2½–3 hours. Serve with heated gooseberry jelly.

Serves 6.

HELSTON PUDDING

The Furry or Floral Dance is of Saxon origin, another of the festivals to usher in the summer. The first dance, which takes place at 6.30 or 7 a.m., is called the 'Workers' dance, and takes place before breakfast: after breakfast there is a children's dance of 250 couples at 10 a.m., then at 12 noon a full dress dance, the men wearing top hats, morning coats, and with lily of the valley in their buttonholes. The Furry dancers must enter the shops and houses by the front door and exit by the back. Certain dwellings are marked out beforehand and it is considered good fortune to be chosen. The dancers continue for about an hour, then have ten minutes rest, before they dance back up the steep hill of Helston's main street. The four dances comprise fourteen miles in all: there are two bands, one in the middle and one at the back. All the members of the band also wear lily of the valley sprays. Formerly lunch was served at the Angel Hotel and there was a garden party. The dance is still performed annually on May 8th.

> *'Jan said to me wan day,*
> *Can you dance the Flora?*
> *Iss, I can, with a nice young man,*
> *Off we go to Trora' [Truro].*

HELSTON PUDDING

2 oz. ($\frac{1}{2}$ cup) each of raisins and currants
2 oz. ($\frac{1}{4}$ cup) sugar
2 oz. ($1\frac{1}{4}$ cups) fresh bread-crumbs
2 oz. ($\frac{1}{2}$ cup) flour
a pinch of salt
2 tablespoons ground rice
2 tablespoons grated suet
$\frac{1}{2}$ teaspoon each of mixed spice and bicarbonate of soda
6 tablespoons milk
1 tablespoon finely chopped peel

Dissolve the soda in the milk, mix all the dry ingredients together and then add the soda and milk. Pour into a well-greased basin, cover with greased paper, and either boil (with hot water up to the brim) or steam for 2 hours.

Serves 4-6.

It is good served with LEMON SAUCE: boil 6 oz. ($\frac{3}{4}$ cup) sugar with $\frac{1}{8}$ pint water for 5 minutes, then remove from the heat and add 2 teaspoons of butter and 1 tablespoon lemon juice. Stir until the butter is melted and pour over the top of the pudding.

The Furry Dance, Helston, Cornwall, May 1907, led by Sir William Treloar, then Lord Mayor of London.

A FRICACEE OF VEAL

Minterne is near to Cerne Abbas where the famous Cerne Giant is cut in the chalk of the hillside above the village. The origin of this 180-foot fertility figure, armed with a club, is obscure, but an interesting paper written in 1889 suggests it is a memorial to Corinaeus (a Trojan prince who, according to legend, settled with his followers in this part of Britain) who slew a giant called Goetmagot. In this supposition may also be found the origin of the figures Gog and Magog at the Guildhall in London, and the Salisbury Giant, see page 8. St. Austin's Well, known as the Wishing Well, nearby, is said to work wondrous cures.

A Fricacee of Veal, adapted from *The Closet Opened* (1677) by Sir Kenelme Digby (1603–65), remarkable scientist and writer. Sir Kenelme was the first person to explain the necessity of oxygen to the existence of plants. He wrote many books, and *The Closet Opened*, which was published after his death, is a trove of cures, physics and recipes.

3 lb. chopped lean veal without bone	½ pint (1 cup) white wine
3 medium sliced onions	3 egg yolks
1 pint (2 cups) stock or water	2 oz. (¼ cup) butter
a pinch each of thyme, marjoram and parsley	4 tablespoons cream
20 whole white peppercorns	juice of 1 orange
4 cloves	parsley to garnish

Put the veal, onions, herbs, peppercorns, cloves and stock into a saucepan, bring to the boil, and simmer for about 2 hours or until tender. Season to taste, strain (but reserve stock) and keep hot. In a double boiler put the butter, the veal stock, the wine, some more herbs, and bring to the boil, letting it reduce rapidly for about 10 minutes. Meanwhile beat up the egg-yolks with the cream and add them gradually to the sauce, seeing that it gets thick but does not curdle. Stir well all the time. Then add the veal, stirring it very well until it is all incorporated and hot. Just before serving add a good squeeze of orange juice.

Serves 6.

Chicken can also be cooked this way.

My Lady Holmeby's Receipt to make Mustard (from *The Closet Opened*). Choose true mustard seed; dry it in an oven after the bread is out. Beat and searse it to a subtle powder. Mingle sherry-sack with it stirring it a long time very well so much as to have it of fit consistence for mustard. Then put a good quantity of sugar to it, as 5 or 6 spoonfuls to a pint of mustard. Stir and incorporate all well together. Some do like to put to it a little (but a little) of very sharp wine-vinegar.

Skating at Minterne House, Minterne Magna, Dorset, 1901, the home of Lord and Lady Digby

JUGGED HARE

Dunster Castle is on a high tor above the picturesque village with its seventeenth-century yarn-market in the main street. Part of the fortifications of Dunster Castle date from 1070. William de Mohun started the building on the site of a Saxon fortress. It is still inhabited and has been the home of the Luttrell family since 1376.

Near by is Exmoor, over 250 square miles of wild, peaty moorland where archaeologists have uncovered evidence of human occupation from the Neolithic, the Bronze and Iron ages, and the Roman period. Red deer and semi-wild ponies roam these acres and are the descendants of the wild horses first domesticated by the Celts before the arrival of the Romans. This is the country of Richard Blackmore's Lorna Doone; of ravens, hares, woodcock and curlew; and in the late summer, of whortleberries (the same family as blueberries) which make delicious pies, or when ripe can be eaten with cream and sugar. On the last Sunday in August at the Triscombe Revel, the pickers had 'wort-pie' with cream. If you could eat it without smiling or speaking when teased it meant a lucky fruit season.

Jugged Hare was traditional fare for Boxing Day dinner, served with redcurrant jelly.

'. . . Regarded as food, a jugged hare may be said to crown most others.' Eden Phillpotts.

MARINADE FOR THE HARE

2 tablespoons olive oil	6 crushed juniper berries
1 glass red wine or cider	a sprig of rosemary
1 glass wine vinegar or cider vinegar	2 bayleaves
1 sliced onion or shallot	salt and pepper

Joint the hare (which should be young and hung for at least 3-4 days) and put into the marinade for at least 4 hours or overnight. Note: If cooking for a small family cut off the legs and use those for the jugged hare. The body, or saddle, can be wrapped in bacon rashers and roasted for about 1½ hours and served with hot cooked red cabbage as a vegetable.

6 slices raw ham or bacon	2 heaped tablespoons flour
2 medium sliced onions or 10 small onions	salt and black pepper
1 celery heart	water or hare stock to cover
3 carrots	3 tablespoons redcurrant jelly
2 bayleaves	1 wineglass port or red wine
1 tablespoon chopped parsley and thyme	¼ pint hare blood (optional) or 1 tablespoon creamed cornflour (optional)
4 tablespoons oil	

Take the hare joints from the marinade and dry them slightly. Heat the oil in a large pan and brown them all over. Transfer to an oven-proof dish which has a bed of the vegetables at the bottom and put the ham slices on top. Scatter over the herbs and flour and see that it coats the ingredients. Season to taste, then add hare stock or water to barely cover, and top up with the marinade. Cover, and cook in a moderate oven (300°F.) for about 3 hours. Half an hour before it is ready add the wine and the jelly and stir. Add 1 tablespoon creamed cornflour (cornstarch) if you want a thicker gravy. If using the hare blood, remove the joints and stir in, reheat but do not reboil.

Dunster, Somerset, with the seventeenth century yarn-market and Dunster Castle in the background, c. 1875

MAHOGANY

'I like Cornwall very much. It is not England. It is bare and dark and elemental, Tristan's land . . . It is old, Celtic, pre-Christian.' D. H. Lawrence, Letters.

St Michael's Mount is thought to be the 'Island of Ictis' where merchants from the Mediterranean obtained tin in the first century B.C. The priory on the Mount used to belong to the Breton abbey of Mont St Michel, but subsequently passed into the St Aubyn family. Mount's Bay was notorious in the eighteenth and early nineteenth centuries for the gangs of 'wreckers' who would strip a foundering ship and her crew, often murdering them in the process. The bullion was stealthily but rapidly carried off to hiding places on ponies, some of which were greased and trained to kick to avoid capture. Smuggling was a gentler art, unless the gangs were interfered with. Many of the beer houses, known as 'kiddley-winks', sold contraband brandy, rum and Geneva gin at very cheap prices. Coves along the Cornish coast, called 'Wine', or 'Pepper', give an indication of the cargoes lured onto the rocks.

Mahogany or Blackstrap, is a favourite drink of Cornish fishermen. Dr Johnson and Boswell were at a dinner given by Sir Joshua Reynolds in 1781 and were served it. Boswell wrote afterwards: 'I thought it very good liquor: a counterpart of what is called Atholl Porridge in the Highlands of Scotland, which is a mixture of whisky and honey!'

It is a mixture of 2 parts gin and 1 part treacle (molasses) beaten very well together.

CORNISH PUNCH

1 bottle Jamaica rum
½ bottle cognac
1 tumbler (1 cup) lemon juice
boiling water
1 whole lemon rind in the piece
2 lb. (4 cups) sugar
a dash of Benedictine

Put the sugar, lemon juice and rind in a gallon jug, add the cognac and rum, and fill up with boiling water poured from a height. Finally, stir in the Benedictine.

This very old recipe was used at Levant Mine for many generations, and comes from Lambourne.

The 'Eastern Green' driven ashore in Mount's Bay, Marazion, Cornwall, c. 1880; St Michael's Mount in the background

ELVERS

Elvers (eel-fry) are a speciality of Severnside, particularly at Epney, whence elvers are sent to Holland, Austria, Poland and Russia to stock rivers. They are young eels about 2 inches long which come up the Severn on the high spring tides from the spawning grounds in the Sargasso Sea, up the little streams and rivers of Gloucestershire and Somerset. Keynsham in Somerset is famous for Elver cakes and all over Gloucestershire Elver suppers are served around the end of March, but the season can go on for several weeks depending on the weather and tides. The elver shoal looks like a mass of jelly swimming in the water and they should only be eaten when they are still transparent and plump, never when the skin has darkened. They were one of the seasonal delicacies which contributed to the originality and elegance of eighteenth century Bath. A West Country witchcraft story has it that a Somerset woman moved to a nearby county; her grandson was a train driver and brought her up a bucket of elvers. She was seen to take a pail of clear water and set it upon the fire, yet half an hour later she was enjoying a fish dinner, which the cat also enjoyed!

ELVERS AS COOKED IN EPNEY

1 lb. (about 500) elvers

3 rashers fat bacon

2 eggs

a dash of vinegar or lemon juice

Wash the elvers well in salted water, two or three times, then drain well. Heat the bacon and let the fat run out. Remove the bacon, then add the elvers and fry until they become milky, like the white of a fried egg. Do not overcook as this destroys the fine flavour. Beat up the eggs and stir into the mixture and when it is all evenly cooked serve up with the bacon rashers, salt and pepper and the vinegar or lemon. Bread and butter is usually eaten with this dish.

ELVER CAKE

Elver Cake is made in the same way, but a pinch of fresh herbs and a little onion juice are added. It is turned into a dish and pressed down till set and cold, then it is turned out and cut into slices.

In Keynsham, after being very well washed in salted, hot water, elvers are seasoned with herbs and salt and pepper, then wrapped in short crust pastry (the edges moistened to stop the juice escaping) like a Cornish pasty (page 108), and baked in a medium oven (375°F.) for about 20-30 minutes.

Eel Catcher on the Severn,
Gloucestershire, c. 1900

BRAISED BEEF WITH PRUNES STUFFED WITH WALNUTS

J. Stringfellow was a Somerset man who built a successful flying model aeroplane in 1847 and a second model in 1868 which was on view at the Aeronautical Society of Great Britain's exhibition at the Crystal Palace. It won the £100 prize for its light and compact engine.

The neighbourhood of the Vale of Pewsey, Somerset is famous for its walnut trees.

3 lb. lean, stewing beef, cut into convenient serving pieces
1 tablespoon dripping or 2 tablespoons oil
1 heaped tablespoon flour
4 cloves
1 large sliced onion

1 clove garlic, chopped
½ pint (1 cup) dark beer or stout
1 cup soaked, partly cooked and stoned prunes, *or* a can of prunes
approximately 12 walnuts
salt and pepper

Heat the fat or oil and fry the beef pieces in it, on both sides, then add the onion and let it soften. Shake the flour over and mix well, then add the cloves, garlic, salt and pepper and the beer. Let it bubble up and if the sauce seems a little too thick add about ½ cup of water or stock. Put into a casserole, cover and braise in a slow to moderate oven (250°F.) for 2 hours. A half an hour before it is ready, put the walnut halves into the prunes and add them to the braised beef. Leave the lid off and continue cooking.

Serves 4-6.

This recipe is also excellent for pork chops, and if a rabbit is cooked in this way it tastes very like a pheasant.

Early aviators in Somerset, c. *1910*

BADMINTON EGGS

Wiltshire and Hampshire are both hunting grounds for truffles, and as late as the 1930s they were collected in the woods for export. Morels, which are a variety of truffle, are still found. They resemble knobs of deep brown honeycomb on hollow, short white stems. When dried they resemble wrinkled thimbles, and they are delicious in stews or pies. If you find one morel then look for more, for they sometimes spring up in quantity on chalky soil.

Certain dogs are attracted by the strong smell of this underground tuber-like fungus, and can be trained to hunt for it. Notice the slip collar in the photograph which tightens to prevent the dogs eating their find, and also the pointed stick used for digging the truffles up. The animals are always given a small reward after locating this treasure. The whereabouts of truffles is also sometimes indicated by a swarm of small yellow flies which hover over a spot where truffles are present.

6 hard-boiled eggs
6 mushrooms, simmered in wine vinegar for 5 minutes
2 cooked truffles (canned will do)
¼ pint (½ cup) stock
1 tablespoon mushroom ketchup
2 tablespoons port wine
1 tablespoon butter rolled with 1 level tablespoon flour
salt and pepper
3 tablespoons fried breadcrumbs
cayenne pepper

Shell the eggs and cut them in half lengthways, take out the yolks and put into a basin, then put the egg-white cases into a dish. Mash up the yolks with the drained chopped mushrooms and chopped truffles, put into a saucepan with the stock, ketchup, salt, pepper and the port. Let the mixture simmer together for about 15 minutes, then add the *beurre manié* (the butter rolled in flour), and stir well while it thickens the sauce. Fill the egg-whites with the fried crumbs, dust them lightly with cayenne pepper, then pour over the sauce. Serve hot with thin buttered toast.

Serves 3.

Truffle hunter with dogs, Winterslow, Wiltshire,
c. *1870*

ARTICHOKE PIE

This is an Elizabethan recipe which was very popular, although in those days it was made with the bottoms of globe artichokes, as the Jerusalem artichoke did not arrive in these islands until the seventeenth century from North America. In fact this pie can be made with both kinds of artichoke. However, the once common and very cheap globe artichoke is now much more expensive than the other kind, so this recipe uses the Jerusalem variety.

If using the *fonds* or bottoms of globe artichokes, substitute the béchamel sauce with a glass of dry white wine.

Artichoke pie is delicious served with underdone roasted beef or lamb, in which case no other vegetable is needed.

1 lb. Jerusalem artichokes	½ pint (1 cup) milk, warmed
2 hard-boiled eggs	1 heaped tablespoon butter
¼ lb. seedless white grapes	1 heaped tablespoon flour
12 pitted dates	1 tablespoon sherry
salt and pepper	8oz. shortcrust pastry, see page 54

First make the pastry and leave it to chill. Then peel the artichokes and soak them for about 10 minutes in cold water which has had a squeeze of lemon juice or wine vinegar added. This prevents their discolouring. Drain the artichokes and cut them so that they are all about the same size, then cook them in boiling salted water for about 15 minutes until they are soft but in no way mushy. Strain and leave to drain. Melt the butter in a saucepan, stir in the flour, and let it cook for 1 minute, then gradually add the warmed milk, stirring all the time to avoid lumps. When it is smooth add the sherry and stir again. Put the artichokes, grapes, dates (cut in half) into the sauce, heat up and season to taste. Meanwhile let the eggs be cooking, then run them in cold water and remove the shells. Put the artichoke mixture into a deep pie-dish (about 8 inches long) slice the eggs on top, and damp the pie-dish edges with water. Roll out the pastry to the required size and put the pastry lid on, pressing down the edges and notching with a fork. Brush over with milk and bake in a hot oven (400°F.) for about 30 minutes.

Serves 4.

Produce of the vegetable garden, Lacock Abbey, Wiltshire, c. 1843; photograph by W. H. Fox Talbot

GINGERBREAD

'*Hokey-Pokey*
Penny a lump,
That's the stuff
To make you jump.'

'Hokey-Pokey' is thought to be the English corruption of 'Ecco un poco',
as after the Risorgimento, all the ice-cream sellers in England were
Italian.
All over the West Country Fairs are popular, the most famous being
Widecombe Fair, which is possibly the oldest in England. Spiced ale and
gingerbread are traditional, as well as a tug-of-war, the winners getting
a huge cup filled with beer.

'*Tom Pearse, Tom Pearse, lend me thy grey mare,*
All along, down along, out along, lee.
For I want to go to Widecombe Fair,
Wi' Bill Brewer, Jan Stewer, Peter Gurney,
Peter Davey, Dan'l Whiddon, Harry Hawk,
Old Uncle Tom Cobbleigh and all,
Old Uncle Tom Cobbleigh and all.'

6 oz. (1½ cups) flour
5 oz. (⅔ cup) butter
1 teaspoon ground ginger

6 oz. (⅔ cup) brown sugar
6 oz. (⅔ cup) treacle (molasses)
a pinch of bicarbonate of soda
   dissolved in 1 tablespoon milk

Mix together the sugar, slightly warmed butter and the treacle until creamy. Sieve the flour and ginger together, and add, mixing in lightly. Warm the milk and dissolve the soda in it and mix thoroughly into the rest. Well grease a baking sheet, and with floured hands divide the gingerbread mixture into small pieces and place them several inches apart on it. Bake in a moderate to hot oven (375°F.) for about 15 minutes or until crisp.

SPICED ALE

1 quart ale
4 cloves
a pinch of mixed spice

2 large peeled and sliced apples
½ teaspoon nutmeg
1 teaspoon sugar

Heat the ale slowly until it is very hot, but on no account let it boil. Add the ingredients and stir well. Let it infuse on the side of the stove for 10 minutes, then strain, but serve with a slice of apple in each tankard.

The 'Hokey-Pokey Man' selling ice cream at a fair, Devon, c. 1908

CORNISH PASTIES

'Crib' is the local name for food in Cornwall: at harvest time it is called 'croust'. Cornish pasties were the most convenient fare, and each one was baked with an initial in the corner: the pasty is started at the opposite corner so that if the meal is interrupted, the owner knows which is his!
'Then we went to a pastry cook's and bought some Cornish "pasties" for lunch, a sort of turnover with meat and potatoes inside, instead of fruit or preserve.'

Francis Kilvert's Diary.

Pasties have been the staple food in Cornwall for centuries: almost any food can be put in the pastry crust, such as fish, bacon, vegetables (especially leeks), herbs, egg or fruit. Legend has it that the devil never crossed the Tamar into Cornwall because, 'fearing they might take a fancy to a devilly pie, he took himself back in Devonshire'.

MEAT PASTY
1 lb. shortcrust pastry (see page 54)
FILLING

1 lb. lean, trimmed, finely chopped beef or lamb (the meat should be raw)	salt and pepper
	1 medium, finely chopped onion
2 medium sized finely chopped raw potatoes	1 tablespoon chopped fresh herbs

Roll out the pastry on a floured board to ¼-inch thick, and cut into four dessert-plate size circles. On each half circle put a layer of the potato, onion, herbs and meat, all well seasoned. Damp the edges and fold over, pressing the edges well, and crimping them between finger and thumb where they join. Make a small slit in the top to let the steam escape. Lay on a baking sheet and bake, first in a hot oven (400°F.) until the pastry is pale gold, then reduce the heat to 350°F. for about 40 minutes. The tops can be brushed with beaten egg or milk when the oven is lowered if a glaze is liked. They are excellent served hot, but also make very good picnic fare if cold.
Makes 4.

'...then they came back and spent the fore-part of the evening over the eggy-hot, down to Oliver's kiddley-wink [beerhouse]...'
My Grandfather, Hendry Watty, Q's Shorter Stories.

EGGY'OT (emphasis on the last syllable) is 2 eggs beaten with 2 tablespoons sugar, then 1 quart of hot beer is poured over the top and stirred briskly.

SAMPSON, another Cornish favourite, is the same, but made with hot cider, and very good for curing a cold.

Eating Cornish pasties at 'Crib' time, near Truro, Cornwall, 1905

ST CATHERINE'S CAKES

The art of pillow lace-making was brought to Devon in the latter half of the sixteenth century by Flemish refugees from the Spanish persecutions; many names of Flemish origin are still to be found in Honiton and other districts of East Devon. Previously only needle lace had been made by nuns, but the Flemings introduced the bobbin and very fine thread. It was originally known as 'bone' lace, for the bobbins were made from sheep's trotters, and fish bones were used to pin the lace to the cushion. The introduction of machinery dealt a lethal blow to lace-making, but all lovers of beautiful handcraft should support this dying art.

St Catherine is the patron saint of lacemakers, and her feast day, 24th November, is still upheld in parts of Devon and Somerset. Somehow St Catherine has been connected with the banished Catherine of Aragon, for she lived in many different places all over England when Anne Boleyn came into favour. One of them was Ampthill, in Bedfordshire, where lace was also made. In Somerset it is known as 'Cattern's Eve' and the 'Cattern' cakes, shaped like Catherine wheels, are made from spiced pastry with currants in it. They are eaten hot with mulled ale, and later cider is drunk. A Cattern-tide Feast is held with hot pork chops decorated with apple rings and ivy. St Catherine's Day is said to usher in the winter.

8 oz. (2 cups) plain flour
1 level teaspoon bicarbonate of soda
8 oz. (1 cup) butter
8 oz. (1 cup) sugar
a pinch of mixed spice
2 heaped tablespoons ground almonds
2 heaped tablespoons currants or seedless raisins
1 beaten egg

Mix together the flour, spice, bicarbonate of soda, sugar and ground almonds. Melt the butter and stir in, mixing to a stiff paste. Then add the currants or raisins and finally the well-beaten egg. Mix very thoroughly; the paste will be quite stiff. Turn out on to a floured board or table and roll out to $\frac{1}{4}$-inch thickness. Cut into $\frac{1}{4}$-inch strips about 8 inches long, and roll round like a Catherine wheel, moistening with a little cold water to make the paste stick. Put onto a greased baking sheet, and bake in a hot oven (400°F.) for 10-15 minutes. If preferred they can be simply cut out like small biscuits, but the wheel shape is traditional. They will keep for some time in an airtight tin.

Makes about 20.

Mrs Woodgate, Honiton, Devon, lace-maker, who
helped to make Queen Victoria's Coronation dress

MARINATED WEST COUNTRY MACKEREL

This recipe can also be used for herrings and pilchards, and is exceptionally good, giving the fish a most delicate flavour.

8 cleaned mackerel
8 bayleaves
20 black peppercorns

1 tablespoon brown sugar
½ pint (1 cup) of equal parts of white vinegar and cold milk-less tea

Lay the cleaned and split mackerel, with a bayleaf inside each one, side by side in an ovenproof dish. Sprinkle over the brown sugar and peppercorns evenly and finally pour over the mixed vinegar and cold tea. Cover with foil, and bake in a moderate oven (350°F.) for about ¾-1 hour. Leave to get cold in the juice, and serve cold, when the liquid will be lightly jellied. A delicious first course, or for a light meal.

Serves 4.

POTTED HERRINGS
also for mackerel or pilchards

4 fresh cleaned herrings
4 oz. (½ cup) butter
a pinch of cayenne pepper
melted butter to finish

½ teaspoon powdered mace
a little salt and pepper
1 cup cider

Bake the cleaned fish in the cider for about ½ hour, then let them cool slightly and remove all the bones and skin. Mash the fish well and put the flesh into a saucepan with all the other ingredients and 2 tablespoons of the fish juice. Heat up, stirring well so that it is all well mixed and when scalded remove from the heat. Put the paste into a pot when cold, and pour the melted butter over the top. Let it get completely cold before using. This paste will keep for some time in a cold place, so long as the top is airtight with the butter. Eat at once when the butter seal has been opened. Serve with toast.

Enough for about 4.

'Trip in the Bay', Weston-super-Mare, Somerset, c. *1893*

MADEIRA CAKE

was so called because it was originally made to be eaten with a glass of Madeira wine. Bristol has been an important wine centre since Norman times, and is in fact built on a catacomb-like maze of wine cellars. A writer of Norman times describes the city as 'the most opulent city in these parts'. Bristol Milk and Bristol Cream are two sherries which are world famous, and 'Milk' has been used for centuries as a synonym for dessert sherry. Fuller, in his History of the Worthies of England, *writes: 'though as many elephants are fed as cows grazed within the walls of this city, yet great plenty of this Metaphorical Milk, whereby Xeres or Sherry-sack is intended is consumed . . . Some will have it called Milk because . . . such Wine is the first moisture given infants in this city. It is also the entertainment of course, which the courteous Bristolians present to all strangers, when visiting their city.' This habit brought forth Edward VII's famous phrase 'All I can say is you've got fine cows'!*

6 oz. (¾ cup) butter
8 oz. (1 cup) caster (extrafine) sugar
finely grated rind of 1 small lemon

10 oz. (2½ cups) sifted self-raising flour
⅛ pint (¼ cup) milk
4 beaten eggs
1 thin slice candied lemon peel

First line a 7-inch cake tin (preferably one with a removable base) with buttered and floured wax paper. Thoroughly cream the butter with the lemon rind until light and fluffy, then fold in the sugar and cream again very well. Add a quarter of the flour and about 1 egg at a time, beating well after each addition. Then stir in the milk and beat again. Pour into the prepared cake tin and bake just below the middle of the oven at a temperature of 345°F. for about 1 hour, then add the very finely sliced piece of candied lemon peel, and continue cooking for about another 15 minutes. Unless you have a really heavy iron baking sheet, put the cake tin on a thick fold of brown paper. Leave until the sides just shrink away from the tin before removing to cool.

Makes about a 2-pound cake.

Wine and cake in the garden of Rupert House, Bristol, c. 1865

GOLD AND SILVER CAKES

The Maypole and the choosing of the 'May Queen' took place on 1st May and was always a public holiday enjoyed by young and old alike, who went 'a-Maying': bringing back flowers and branches of trees, the centre of attraction being the Maypole, which was usually made of birch wood decorated with ribbons. The origin can be traced back to ancient times and is connected with the goddess Flora and fertility for the coming year. Until the turn of the century, chimney sweeps used to lead about a 'Jack-i'-the-Green'—a chimney sweep boy enveloped in boughs.

Gold and Silver Cakes were a great favourite of Queen Victoria.

SILVER CAKES

4 oz. (½ cup) butter	5 stiffly-beaten egg-whites
4 oz. (½ cup) caster (extrafine) sugar	1 heaped teaspoon baking powder
	1 teaspoon almond essence
6 oz. (1½ cups) sifted flour	2 tablespoons ground almonds

Cream the butter and sugar thoroughly, then add the flour and egg-whites in alternate spoonfuls, mixing well. Add the almond essence and the ground almonds and finally the baking powder, seeing that it is all well-mixed. Put into greased patty tins or a baking sheet, and bake in a moderate oven for about 15 minutes or until risen and golden. This mixture, studded with fruit or nuts just before baking, makes excellent *petit fours*.

GOLD CAKE

4 oz. (½ cup) butter	5 well beaten egg-yolks
4 oz. (½ cup) caster (extrafine) sugar	2 teaspoons baking powder
	4 tablespoons whisky, orange or
6 oz. (1½ cups) sifted flour	lemon juice

Cream the butter and sugar, and make exactly the same as Silver Cake except using the egg-yolks instead of whites, and the whisky, orange or lemon juice in place of the ground almonds and almond essence. Bake as above, but increase the cooking time to 20 minutes, or until risen and golden.

Both cake mixtures can be cooked in 5-6-inch cake tins for 50-60 minutes if a whole cake is required.

Children at the Maypole, Gloucestershire, c. 1900

ROAST STUFFED GOOSE

'There was meals, roasted chickens, an' a tongue, an' a great ham. There was cheese-cakes that she made after a little secret of her own; an' a bowl of junket an inch deep in cream, that bein' his pet dish; an' all kinds o' knick-knacks, wi' grapes an' peaches an' apricots, an' decanters o' wine, white and red.' The Drawn Blind, *Q's Shorter Stories.*

'At Tregarrick Fair they cook a goose in twenty-two different ways...' *Ibid.*

1 10-lb. goose	1 pint (2 cups) dry, draught cider
FOR THE STUFFING	
6 large peeled, cored and sliced apples soaked in rum for 4 hours	1 large chopped onion
	the chopped goose liver
	salt and pepper
3 finely chopped sage leaves	4 oz. (1 cup) sausage meat
a pinch of nutmeg or mace	4 oz. (1 cup) mashed potato
3 cups breadcrumbs	

Mix all ingredients except the sausage meat and potato together and stuff into the body of the bird. In the crop end put an equal mixture of sausage meat and cooked, mashed potato, approximately 4 oz. of each, well seasoned. These amounts are enough for a 10-12 lb. bird.

Put the bird on a low rack in the baking tin with very little oil or dripping, just over the legs and wings. Cover with foil and roast in a moderate oven, 350°F., for 20 minutes to the pound and allow 20 minutes over. Baste every half-hour with warm, dry, draught cider, and after 1 hour prick the breast to allow the juices to run out. Remove the foil for the last quarter of an hour, and when done put the bird onto a warmed serving dish. Pour off any excess fat, boil up the pan juices on top of the stove, adding 1 level tablespoon dry mustard powder, salt, a squeeze of lemon and orange juice, and about 1 cup of giblet stock. Let this bubble up, and serve separately. When the goose is at table, heat a small ladle-full of rum, pour over the bird and set light to it. Apple sauce is unnecessary with this magnificent dish.

Many pubs in Cornwall made, and still make, their own beer. The Blue Anchor at Helston makes an excellent stingo.

'Loan blethan noueth,	*'A Happy New Year,*
halbennen joungk	*And a young woman,*
ha mona lour gans goz Gureg'	*And plenty of money with your wife'*

A Cornish New Year Greeting

INDEX